*To the missionaries and members of The Church of
Jesus Christ of Latter-day Saints in the Netherlands,
Belgium, and the Salt Lake Brighton Stake.
May they always be true in defining moments!*

"There are certain mortal moments and minutes that matter—certain hinge points in the history of each human. Some seconds are so decisive they shrink the soul, while other seconds are spent so as to stretch the soul."

Elder Neal A. Maxwell

(*Deposition of a Disciple* [Salt Lake City: Deseret Book, 1976], 77.)

◆　◆　◆　◆　◆　◆　◆　◆　◆　◆

CONTENTS

* * * * * * * * * *

PREFACE

✦ ✦ ✦ ✦ ✦ ✦ ✦ ✦ ✦ ✦

While each decision we make has an ultimate bearing on our future opportunities and blessings, certain pivotal points are critical. In these soul-defining moments, we are faced with choices that once made will, in many cases, forever open or close doors of opportunity.

History records the positive and negative results of choices that were made in defining moments of such earthly and eternal consequence—moments that mattered so very much. Adam and Eve's *choice* to partake of the forbidden fruit and thus effectuate the plan that would bring each of us to earth was a hinge point of history. The scriptures remind us that "Adam fell that men might be; and men are, that they might have joy" (2 Nephi 2:25).

Esau's decision to sell his birthright for a bowl of beans (pottage), in order to satisfy a short-lived physical craving, not only showed shortsightedness on his part but also had lasting effects on his potential posterity. Members of The Church of Jesus Christ of Latter-day Saints are today the children of Jacob (Israel) rather than of Esau (see Genesis 25:29–34).

How often in life have we, like Esau, bartered away something of significant, even eternal, value in order to satisfy a short-lived passion, appetite, or desire? Sometimes this bartering is done under the duress of peer pressure, where we are urged to participate in something that is declared as the popular or so-called "in" thing to do, even though it is outside the standards of righteousness set by God or His servants.

Occasionally this bartering away of values occurs in private moments, when we succumb to personal temptation. Choices made in character-defining moments, whether public or private, determine our destiny.

King David's decision not only to pause and watch a woman bathing but also to pursue the evil thoughts spawned in that moment of sin led to his loss of a much more important crown than the one worn on his mortal brow (see 2 Samuel 11; Acts 2:34; D&C 132:39).

Joseph, who was sold into slavery by his jealous brothers, was an example of one who made the right choices regardless of the sometimes unfair consequences. His steadfast refusal to submit to the seductive invitations of his master Potiphar's wife led to her unrighteous rage toward him. Because he stood for what was right in a defining moment, Joseph was unjustly cast into a foul prison for years (see Genesis 39).

Blessings for doing right do not always come immediately. One who stands for the right may sometimes suffer severe persecution or stand outside the *popular* crowd—for a few mortal moments. But the Lord has promised, "If thou endure it well, God shall exalt thee on high; thou shalt triumph over all thy foes" (D&C 121:8).

The prophet Abinadi's unwavering refusal to recant his testimony of Jesus Christ led not only to his own martyrdom but also to the conversion of a young priest named

Alma. In a defining moment, one man's death by fire kindled the flame of faith in another (see Mosiah 12–17).

The following pages cite numerous examples of defining moments when choices—some seemingly small and others more momentous—were so defining in their consequences. I hope that you will be motivated by these experiences to commit to making the *right* decisions in your life—and to make certain choices *now!*

One of the great lessons to be learned from those who have made correct choices is that they have decided on their course of action in advance. They have set their lives on such a proper path that when a moment of decision arrives, their reaction is natural. Thus, if you haven't already done so, make the decision *now* that you will never barter away the standards you know to be true.

In the words of Elder Neal A. Maxwell, of the Quorum of the Twelve Apostles, "Act [or decide] now, so that a thousand years from now, when you look back at this moment, you can say this was a moment that mattered— this was a day of determination" ("Why Not Now?" *Ensign*, Nov. 1974, 13).

Chapter 1

WHAT MAKES HEROES

♦ ♦ ♦ ♦ ♦ ♦ ♦ ♦ ♦ ♦

"Six-Year-Old Boy Saves Mother from Attacker!"

The headline caught many people's attention. The story revealed how a man had broken into a home and threatened the mother with bodily harm. Rising to the challenge of the moment, her young son quickly ran to the hall closet and grabbed an unloaded rifle. Leveling the barrel at the intruder, the boy ordered him to leave the frightened woman alone. Sensing the determination of the boy to save his mother, and not knowing the gun was unloaded, the evil man released the woman and fled.

In a dramatic and momentous moment, an unknown boy became an instant hero.

One of the characteristics heroes seem to share is an ability to forget themselves—their comfort or even their safety—in seeking to help others in distress.

Elder Jacob de Jager, emeritus General Authority, once told a story of courage displayed by some of his native countrymen in Holland years ago. During a severe storm a ship was sinking offshore, and volunteers manned rowboats to rescue the stranded sailors. It took great courage and strength to row through the treacherous waves in reaching the endangered vessel. Although they finally arrived at the ship, they discovered there was not room enough in the small rowboat to take everyone back to the safety of the shore. One man had to remain on board the imperiled ship.

By the time the rescuers made it back to the beach, their strength was spent. Exhaustion had taken its toll, and they could not safely attempt another trip to rescue the stranded sailor on the ship. By this time many spectators had arrived at the scene, and more volunteers were asked for to make a second rescue attempt. Among those stepping forward was a nineteen-year-old Dutch youth named Hans.

The youth's mother pleaded with him not to go, saying, "Your father died at sea when you were four years old, and your older brother Pete has been reported missing at sea for more than three months now. You are the only son left to me!"

The young man's courage did not waver, and he told his mother that he had a duty to help rescue that single soul on the ship. The small rowboat slid into the sea, and once again a battle for life commenced. After what seemed like an eternity to the mother, the rescuers returned. When they were close enough to shore to be heard above the roar of the wind, a man on the beach cupped his hands and shouted through the storm, "Did you save him?"

The crowd on the beach saw the hero Hans rise from his rowing bench and shout back, "Yes! And tell Mother it is my brother Pete!" (Conference Report, Oct. 1976, 81).

Not all heroes have their deeds displayed before an adoring, appreciative public. Nor are the deeds of most heroes as dramatic as that of the brave boy who rescued his mother or the Dutch youth who saved his brother.

In the summer of 1953, a sixteen-year-old was serving as an apprentice actress at a theater in Virginia. She shared a suite of rooms with another young girl who was the lead actress. Every morning when the apprentice woke up, she found the other girl quietly reading in her bed.

The lead actress "was a Mormon, and in an environment where morals simply did not exist, she was as pure as snow. No drinking, no smoking, not even in plays, and no men in her room. She loved everyone, and she was so gentle and friendly even though she was the 'star.' And always in the morning she was reading and reading, not her scripts, but some other books and magazines that she had brought with her."

This Mormon girl was a heroine filled with moral courage in circumstances where the pressure to be otherwise was ever present. Although she never tried to push her beliefs on her roommate or the others, her actions spoke louder than any words. Who knows how many situations were bettered because of her courage to stand for what she knew to be right? Years later her example was still reaping benefits, for her roommate remembered the lifestyle of the Mormon girl and initiated contact with the Church.

Following her baptism and that of her husband, the adult woman said, "I've never been able to find that young lady to tell her that, because she lived her religion in a way that I could not forget, thirty-seven people on both sides of our families are members of the Church. Countless others in the spirit world also have been given the opportunity.

"We never know," she said, "we just never know, who is watching us, and what they are learning from us" (Ann Fowler Lehne, "Comment," *Ensign*, Dec. 1977, 62).

Quiet courage is found daily among a vast array of anonymous heroes. Unknown, unsung, and unheralded—at least in mortality—these heroes are those who are committed to moral integrity. No matter what the circumstances, no matter how strong the social pressure to lower standards, to succumb to sin, to give in to what appears to be the *easy* way, a real hero remains steadfast and true.

Just as the evil intruder fled from the home where a courageous young boy *resisted* him, so will the devil flee from a true hero who resists the evil one's efforts to tempt or mock him or her (see James 4:7).

The morally courageous recognize the lies of Lucifer in such phony phrases as "Nobody will ever know," "Everybody's doing it," or "One time won't matter." These heroes follow the example of Jesus, who "suffered temptations but *gave no heed* unto them" (D&C 20:22; emphasis added).

This principle is also taught in the vision of the tree of life. A contrast is shown between the faithful who kept their eyes riveted on righteousness, never straying from the strait and narrow path leading to the fruit of the tree representing God's love, and the wayward who wandered in *strange roads*. This latter group forsook the road of righteousness and sought to enter a *strange building*, which represented pride, vanity, and the ways of the world (see 1 Nephi 8:26–27, 31–32; 11:35; 12:18).

Upon entering the building, the wayward joined forces with the wicked of the world in mocking the righteous. Nephi's description of this attempt to deride and derail the righteous from the true track is instructive: "Great was the multitude that did enter into that strange building. And after they did enter into that building they did point the finger of scorn at me and those that were partaking of the fruit also; but *we heeded them not.* . . . For as many as heeded them, had fallen away" (1 Nephi 8:33–34; emphasis added).

Heroes give no heed to temptation or to the mockery of those who have slipped and fallen prey to its siren song. In ancient times mariners often claimed to hear the alluring sound of a mythical maid of the deep—a siren. Her bewitching voice lured many seafaring vessels to their destruction on unseen and treacherous reefs.

In our day the siren song of Satan seeks to entice us to reefs that can bring only regret and sorrow. Just as surely as ancient ships sailed to destruction by following the sound of the siren, so in our day will those who follow the sounds of Satan be led to a more devastating destruction—that of their souls.

In moments of mockery, when our righteous efforts are belittled by the small in spirit, it would be well to remember and recite the words of the Apostle Paul, who said, "I am not ashamed of the gospel of Christ: for it is the power of God unto salvation" (Romans 1:16).

It is also helpful to remember the example of a young teenager, the Prophet Joseph Smith. In spite of numerous efforts by scorners to belittle and belie his testimony of truth, he stood firm and immovable (see JS—H 1:21–25).

5

We can all be heroes in the eyes of the Lord by acting courageously in moral matters. The Lord loves a courageous person. Sometimes courage will be demonstrated before crowds; other times it will be seen by only one or two. Yet, on other occasions, no mortal eyes will witness the moral courage or spiritual strength displayed in private defining moments that matter so much—those personal moments when we are alone with our thoughts and actions and only unseen eyes beyond the veil are watching.

Sometimes these private moments are filled with more drama than others. Take the example of Ruben Dario Pacheo of Caracas, Venezuela. He and his family had been diligently saving money to take a trip to the nearest temple in order to participate in those holy ordinances that would seal them eternally as an inseparable family. He sent his daughter to the bank to withdraw the $500 in United States currency that they had saved for the trip. She brought the money home in an envelope, and her mother, without counting the contents, placed it in a safe place.

The night before the family left, the father checked the contents of the money and found that the bank had given them $4,065 instead of the $500 requested and listed on the receipt. The bank had given them an extra $3,565, for which there was no record. If it was to be returned, the action would be strictly voluntary, for the bank was unaware of where the money had gone.

Ruben Dario Pacheo, a member of The Church of Jesus Christ of Latter-day Saints, was about to take his family to visit one of the most holy places on earth—the temple of God. How could he enter that sacred sanctuary with a stained character? He knew what was right. More important, he had the courage to act on that knowledge. The money was returned. Brother Pacheo was a true hero (see Mario G. Echeverri, "Venezuela," *Ensign*, Feb. 1977, 30).

Most of us will never face that kind of decision. Few will have a bank error give them thousands of dollars in excess of what is rightfully theirs. How many, however, will face the decision of whether to return excess "pocket change" mistakenly received in a minor business transaction? Is there any difference in courage and cowardice if the money involved is small or great?

Years ago Elder Sterling W. Sill told of a decision he had to make when a pop machine gave him a *free* drink. He could have walked away with a couple of extra coins in his pocket but chose to do otherwise. "Why should I become a thief for pennies?" he said to himself. "I wouldn't take money from the owner's money till or wallet; why should I take it from his vending machine?" The amount of money taken dishonestly makes no difference. A true hero remains courageous whether he is fighting fierce dragons representing major temptations or pesky, irritating smaller baits or bribes.

Each of us can be a hero of righteousness. A simple formula for being such a hero was given many years ago to one who possessed physical but, more important, moral courage: "Only be thou strong and *very* courageous, that thou mayest observe to do according to all the law, . . . turn not from it to the right hand or to the left" (Joshua 1:7; emphasis added).

Chapter 2

THE VOICE OF ONE

* * * * * * * * * *

"Let our voices be heard," admonished Elder Gordon B. Hinckley. "I hope they will not be shrill voices, but I hope we shall speak with . . . conviction" (Conference Report, Oct. 1975, 58).

It is cowardice, unbecoming of one who professes to follow the Perfect Pattern, even Jesus Christ, to stand silent while others perpetuate falsehoods or succumb to sin. The voice of a faithful friend giving a clear signal can be a source of strength, support, and solace in moments that give definition to one's character.

Consider the personal experience of one young basketball player who, together with his teammates, accepted an invitation to a party following their state championship victory. They were all invited to the home of one of the school's cheerleaders to celebrate.

"We found that the girl's parents were gone over the weekend, and that she had invited exactly twelve girls to her home as well as the team. She soon rolled the rug back and had the stereo going. They turned it up loud, and then the girl who was the hostess went into the kitchen and came out with a carton of cigarettes. She threw a package over to the fellow who was sitting on the end, and she said, 'Hey, training's over. We can smoke tonight.'

"Well, we were from a Mormon community. I watched

the first fellow—he took a cigarette. Then the girl next to him took one. So did the girl next to her. And as the cigarettes got closer and closer to me, it seemed that almost everyone there was taking a cigarette.

"It was an embarrassing moment and I didn't know how to handle it.

"Finally I thought, 'Oh well, it's only one cigarette and I guess I can smoke with them.' Anyway, when the cigarettes went to the fellow right next to me, he said, 'No, thanks, I don't smoke,' and passed them on.

"The strength of the friend on my left gave me the courage to do what I really wanted to do all along. I said, 'No, thanks,' too.

"The thing I have wondered through all these years is, what would have happened to me if I had been sitting on *the other side* of my friend?" (Vaughn J. Featherstone, *A Generation of Excellence* [Salt Lake City: Bookcraft, 1975], 169–70).

A significant sermon can be preached in such simple words as, "No, thanks." Yet the impact can have far-reaching consequences. Who is to say what might have been the future of either of the two boys who refused the cigarettes *if* the *one* voice had not spoken first?

Warnings need not come in the form of loud sermons. They can come through the quiet example or a word of encouragement from a committed, courteous, even socially courageous friend.

Years ago a young girl in high school needed such a friend. "She came from a very economically disadvantaged home. There was no money at all, and so consequently her clothes were either remade, hand-me-downs, or gifts from others. They were all remnants—not the same type of clothing most wore. Her shoes were red plastic. . . . After she would wear them a day or two, they would split. Her white socks were never white because of the dirt those holes would let in. She was having a tough time."

Fortunately for the girl, there was a young man in her history class who tried to befriend her. "One day there was a history test and they studied a little bit together. He showed her that he cared, not romantically, but as a friend. She confided to him later that that was the day she had planned to take her own life. She was on her way home to destroy herself. But because he had been kind to her, she had hung on and didn't commit suicide. . . . She is a nurse now and is happy. She is ministering unto the needs of others and very much alive, because someone sitting next to her in class was kind" (Hugh W. Pinnock, "Courage," address at the Salt Lake Institute of Religion, Nov. 11, 1977, 8–9).

How often has each of us had an opportunity to spread sunshine in the lives of others by simply showing an interest in them—by saying "hello" or by offering to walk with them or eat lunch with them? When we enter a room, do we look for ways to make others comfortable, or are we only concerned with our own grand entrance?

Looking beyond ourselves can bring great satisfaction to us and much joy in the lives of others. An encouraging word uttered at the right moment could make a difference in another's day, or even another's life. Failure to act with courage in defining moments can leave lasting scars on the soul.

Contemplate the lesson learned by one young soldier. Following the armistice of World War I, he was visiting the French city of Bordeaux. After a day of sight-seeing, he went to a place in the town square where he was to be picked up and returned to camp. While he was standing in the shadow of a building, another young soldier whom he knew approached the same general area and stood under a dim streetlight. This soldier was soon approached by a young French girl who quickly made her seductive intentions known. The soldier in the shadows watched as the other young man looked around to make certain he was not being observed and then disappeared into the darkness with the girl.

Later the two soldiers were discharged and arrived in their hometown together. The soldier who had stood silently in the shadows observed the other soldier being warmly greeted by a young woman with a baby in her arms—his wife and his daughter. "How could he have betrayed his trust with his loved ones?" the other soldier thought. Yet, later, as he reflected on his role of silence in the shadows, a new thought came to him: "If I had stepped from the shadows and joined him, or called to him, or let him know in any way that I was there he might not have gone with that girl. By a simple act I might have saved him" (S. Dilworth Young, "How the Holy Ghost Can Help You," *New Era*, Oct. 1971, 6).

What is your personal answer to Cain's self-condemning inquiry, "Am *I* my brother's keeper?" (Genesis

4:9; emphasis added). The Lord gave His answer through an Old Testament prophet: If "thou givest [the wicked] not warning, nor speakest to warn the wicked from his wicked way, to save his life; the same wicked man shall die in his iniquity; but his blood will I require at thine hand. . . . If thou warn the righteous man, that the righteous sin not, and he doth not sin, he shall surely live, because he is warned; also thou hast delivered thy soul" (Ezekiel 3:18, 21).

Of what value is the keeper of a lighthouse if he does not keep the light shining steadily to show ships the safety of the harbor and the hazards of an unsafe course? Just as the lighthouse keepers are charged with the safety of sailors and ships, the Savior has likewise charged His Saints to let their lights shine for the spiritual safety of others (see Matthew 5:14–16; D&C 115:5).

One light and one voice can surely make a difference in momentous moments!

Many years ago a young Norwegian widow sent some shoes to a local shoemaker to be repaired. When the repaired shoes were returned, she found that each shoe contained a small religious tract. The shoemaker said to her, "You may be surprised to hear me say that I can give you something of more value than soles for your child's shoes."

The woman was startled and inquired as to the meaning of this statement. The humble shoemaker bore his testimony of the gospel of Jesus Christ and challenged the woman to listen to his message. He was not afraid to open his mouth to share the message of "the great plan of happiness" (Alma 42:8).

The widow's heart was touched. She listened; she learned. "At length, on 1 April 1881, a little more than two years after she first heard of the Gospel, she was baptized into the Church. . . . Thin ice still lay over the edges of the fjord, which had to be broken to permit the [baptism]. The water was icy cold yet she declared to her dying day that never before in all her life had she felt warmer or more comfortable than when she came out of the baptismal waters. . . . The fire within was kindled, never to be extinguished" (John A. Widtsoe, *In the Gospel Net*, 3rd ed. [Salt Lake City: Bookcraft, 1966], 63–69).

Anna Widtsoe's young son John A. followed his mother's example. He too joined the Church and eventually came to America, where he distinguished himself as a secular and spiritual scholar. He became the president of two universities and was called to serve as a member of the Quorum of the Twelve Apostles. His discourses and writings remain as reminders of the faith of the voice of one humble shoemaker in Norway.

Frequently the voice or actions of one with courage can trigger an outpouring on the part of others that rises in a ringing crescendo of righteous conviction. President David O. McKay related the experience of one young man whose conviction to act correctly stirred similar courage on the part of others:

"A young missionary was invited to a wedding in a foreign country, at which two of his acquaintances were joined together in bonds of matrimony, the ceremony being performed by a minister of another church. This young man was the only member of the Mormon church present amidst the one hundred or more guests at the table in the hotel. By each plate was a wine cup, filled to the brim, and also a glass of water. After the ceremony, as the guests were all in their places, the minister arose and said: 'Now I propose that the company drink to the health of the newly married couple.' They all arose. Now propriety suggested that this young man take up the wine in his wine cup. But he was a missionary. He belonged to a Church that preaches a Word of Wisdom. . . . He was preaching that, and he was pretending to live it. Here was a time when he could indulge. No one would know—indeed, it seemed to be the act of propriety, but he resisted. Now was the opportunity to defend his Church, and that is what he did. He took the glass of water. Some of his immediate friends by him, dropping their wine cups, followed his example, and at least half a dozen wine glasses remained untouched. Others saw it, and the circumstance furnished an excellent opportunity to converse with those guests upon the Word of Wisdom.

"Now, was he humiliated? No. He was strengthened. Were the guests embarrassed? No. Did they feel to condemn him? No. Condemnation was replaced by admiration, as it always is in the hearts of intelligent and God-fearing men and women" (Conference Report, Oct. 1958, 92).

One need not be faced with major temptations nor be old in years to successfully face a momentous moment.

Consider the case of an eleven-year-old English girl named Lisa:

"She came home from school one day feeling very excited. She had been asked to read a part in the school devotional assembly the following morning. She said to her mother, 'But some of the words are wrong.' Her mother discovered that one paragraph referred to God and the Holy Ghost as being one and the same person. Lisa and her mother decided to write a letter to Lisa's teacher explaining that this paragraph was contrary to Lisa's belief, and that she would feel much happier leaving it out.

"The next afternoon her mother waited anxiously for Lisa to return home from school. She came home with a big, bright smile on her face. Not only had the teacher let her leave the paragraph out, but she had asked for more information about the Church. In addition, the teacher asked Lisa to present an assembly about the Church. All this came about because Lisa lived up to the covenant she had made and was willing to witness to the world her own beliefs" (Dwan J. Young, "Keeping the Covenants We Make at Baptism," *Ensign*, Nov. 1984, 94).

A thirteen-year-old German boy, Armin Suckow, Jr., also had occasion to raise his voice in defense of truth. He relates his experience as follows:

"We spoke one Christmastime with one of our school teachers about Jesus. He said that after Jesus died, he had gone from the earth and was now dead. As the teacher spoke, I thought about our church and knew that after three days Jesus was resurrected and was seen by many people. Later, then, he ascended into heaven. I had the feeling that I should tell the teacher and the students that the truth was entirely different from what the teacher had just said. The teacher didn't want to hear my opinion at all, but in spite of that, I . . . told them that Jesus was resurrected. It didn't please the teacher at all that I should correct him, but I continued. Then he said that this was simply a matter of opinion. I answered him that anyone can read of this event in the scriptures and that it is so clearly described there that no one can get a different opinion on the story than the one that I had given. After the class the teacher wanted to know to which church I belonged. I told him that I belonged to The Church of Jesus Christ of Latter-day Saints. On that day I had a real good feeling inside of me" ("The Savior Lives!" *New Era*, Dec. 1977, 18).

Occasionally unseen but hearing ears are the benefactors of brave voices that are raised to silence sin. Elder Rex D. Pinegar told of such an incident in his young life:

"One day my older brother, Lynn, came hurrying home from school basketball practice, bringing a teammate with him. Upon entering the house, both made a dash for the kitchen to satisfy their hungry appetites. My brother's friend loudly described his feeling of hunger by using a few vulgar and profane words to accent his anxious mood. Lynn quickly, quietly, but firmly, said, 'Hey, don't talk like that. My little brothers might hear you. I don't want them to learn words like that. Besides, they might think less of you than they ought to.'

"Unknown to my brother, my friend and I did hear that conversation, but the profane words were quickly erased from my mind by the thoughtful concern and courage shown by my older brother. That experience made a positive, lasting impression on my young mind. At the risk of sacrificing a friendship, his kindly chastisement of his friend taught me a lesson of love and concern for others and of courage to uphold the right" (Conference Report, Apr. 1974, 96).

"The finest of friends must sometimes be stern sentinels, who will insist that we become what we have the power to become. The 'no' of such stern sentinels is more to be prized than a 'yes' of others" (Neal A. Maxwell, "Insights from My Life," *1976 Devotional Speeches of the Year* [Provo: BYU Press, 1977], 199).

Several years ago I was one of the passengers on a crowded bus. It was the end of a workday, and people were generally absorbed in their own little world—reading, sleeping, or just staring ahead. Few were engaged in conversation. At one bus stop several boisterous teenagers boarded the bus and proceeded to the rear, where they carried on their rather loud conversation as if they were the only ones present. Most of the passengers seemed to sink a little deeper into their private worlds, trying to ignore the noise.

At once it seemed to be more difficult to tune out the teens' conversation because they commenced using vulgarity. Most tried to ignore the blue haze that now permeated the atmosphere of the bus. I found myself getting more and more uncomfortable and considered going back and asking them to stop using such filthy language. However, I finally determined that it would be better to request help from the bus driver rather than to take matters into my own hands. I left my seat and went to the front of the bus and expressed my concern to the driver. He immediately pulled the bus over to the side of the road, unbuckled his seat belt, and walked to the back of the bus, where he confronted the teens.

They were given an ultimatum to clean up their language or immediately leave the bus. They remained silent throughout the rest of the ride. As individual passengers began to arrive at their destinations, several of them stopped at my seat and thanked me for speaking up. I found I was not the only one offended by the foul language, and most were just waiting for someone to speak up.

I had an interesting postscript to this experience. About a month later I was browsing in a downtown store during my lunch hour when a clerk approached me. "Do you ride the Cottonwood Heights bus?" she inquired. "Why, yes," I responded. "Why do you ask?" She smiled and said, "I thought I recognized you. I just wanted to say thanks for what you did in speaking out against those foul-mouthed boys on the bus."

Now, I don't relate this story to garner plaudits but to illustrate that it takes only one voice to make a difference for good. Perhaps someone else *might* have finally spoken up if I had remained in my seat. But, on the other hand, maybe we all would have continued to be subjected to this attack on our spiritual senses.

Not all who raise their voices in defense of truth will receive recognition or even a thank-you. Few receive medals for displays of moral courage. Yet our desire to do right should not be determined by the size of the observing audience but by principles of truth and righteousness.

Elder Neal A. Maxwell noted the need to be bound by principle rather than publicity:

"They err who, instead of concentrating on commandment keeping and personal spiritual progress, desire sweeping significance and high visibility in the second estate.

"Is it really numbers of people touched at the moment which measure the impact of an individual?" ("Grounded, Rooted, Established, and Settled," *Brigham Young University Fireside and Devotional Speeches* [Provo: BYU Press, 1982], 17).

The *voice of one* really does make a difference!

Chapter 3

THE SOLDIER WHO STOOD BY

* * * * * * * * * *

When the moment of opportunity occurs, the time for preparation is past!

The Book of Mormon relates an episode in the life of the righteous Captain Moroni when his soldiers had surrounded the army of his enemies. Not wishing to shed further blood, Moroni called a halt to his soldiers' fighting and sought for a peaceful settlement with the leader of the opposing army, an evil man named Zerahemnah.

Moroni reminded his foe that the fighting was initiated by Zerahemnah and his followers, who were angry at Moroni's people because of their religion and faith in Christ. Moroni's soldiers sought only to defend their freedom. Moroni asked that his adversaries deliver up their weapons and promise not to make war again.

The wicked Zerahemnah was belligerent in his response. Seeing his present military disadvantage, he agreed to surrender his followers' weapons for the moment, but he would not promise to cease further aggression against those who expressed a faith in Christ.

Seeing no other alternative, Moroni said that this offer was unacceptable and the fighting would be resumed until the wicked were destroyed. Filling with further anger against those who stood for righteousness, the evil Zerahemnah unexpectedly raised his sword and rushed forward to slay the defenseless Moroni, "but as he raised his sword, behold, one of Moroni's soldiers smote it even to the earth" (Alma 44:12).

This soldier is not identified by name. He is simply referred to as *"the soldier who stood by"* (Alma 44:13; emphasis added).

In a critical and defining moment that meant so much to the cause of freedom, an unnamed soldier displayed his preparation for such a moment. Because he *stood by, ready* to respond, his alertness saved the life of his leader and, perhaps, his people as well.

An interesting article appeared in the BYU *Daily Universe* some years ago. The lead paragraph stated, "The quick thinking of several BYU students saved the life of a classmate Thursday morning." The article went on to tell how a student had suddenly slumped over and fallen to the floor of the cafeteria as if he were dead.

Fortunately for this student, there were quick-thinking, alert fellow students who *stood by ready* to render the necessary assistance. A card was found in his wallet stating that he had a heart condition and giving instructions on how to treat him if he should suddenly pass out and appear dead. The instructions were followed, and the young man's heartbeat was restored. The article concluded by stating, "Thanks to his card and alert bystanders he is still alive" ("Phew—That Was a Close One," *Daily Universe*, Apr. 7, 1967, 1).

There were undoubtedly some students who stood around in this emergency, not knowing what to do. A significant difference exists between *standing around* watching and *standing by ready* to act. "Therefore be ye also ready" (Matthew 24:44).

A few years ago a crowd of onlookers stood around and watched with horror as a four-year-old girl lay helpless on the tracks of a subway beneath New York's busy streets. She had slipped from the safety of her mother's grasp and fallen four feet to the tracks below the platform. Only seconds away, an onrushing train could be heard approaching the child with unstoppable fury. Many shouted for someone to save the child but, perhaps frozen with fear, none nearest the scene stepped forward to do so.

About thirty-five feet away, thirty-four-year-old Everett Sanderson saw the pending tragedy. Unable to believe that none made an effort to save the child from the gruesome death that surely awaited her, Sanderson jumped from the platform onto the train tracks and began running toward the child. The lights of the onrushing train could now be seen rapidly advancing in a collision course with the child and her would-be rescuer.

Another who had also leaped onto the tracks to save the girl was even farther away than Sanderson was. Twenty-year-old Miguel Maisonett, seeing that Sanderson was closer to the girl than he was, vaulted back onto the platform and rushed to the spot just above where the girl had fallen. As the black hulk of the train emerged from the tunnel like some hideous, hissing monster ready to devour its victims, Sanderson grabbed the child and with superhuman strength threw her into the outstretched arms of Miguel.

The child was now safe, but Sanderson was in desperate peril of his own life and limbs. Although the motorman had suddenly seen the two on the tracks and applied the brakes, momentum carried the lethal train forward toward its all-but-sure destiny with death. With only a second remaining, Sanderson jumped up toward the platform and happily found himself "rising like an elevator" as Miguel, the child's aunt, and a policeman joined hands in lifting him from the jaws of death. Even as his head and upper torso cleared the platform, however, Sanderson was sure that his legs had been severed by the train. To his joy, he found that he had just made it—thanks to the efforts of the three who *stood by ready* to assist him as he had assisted the child.

When asked if the event had changed his life, Everett Sanderson said, "I don't know whether this has changed my life. I know it almost ended it. But if I hadn't tried to save that little girl, *if I had just stood there like the others*, I would have died inside. I would have been no good to myself from then on" (Warren R. Young, "There's a Girl on the Tracks!" *Reader's Digest*, Feb. 1977, 91–95; emphasis added; used with permission).

Not all defining moments involve such high drama as the subway scene, nor do they involve peril to life and limb. Readiness to act, however, should not be gauged on either its level of dramatic appeal or potential for accolades from an adoring audience.

One high school football player spent most of the season warming the bench, waiting for his moment of action to arrive. Unfortunately, he saw the season slipping by without the moment arriving. Late in one game, he finally gave up hope and decided to take off his tight, uncomfortable shoes. As he sat in his self-pity, the call came. To his chagrin, he heard the coach yell out the young man's name, ordering him into action on the field. The game would not wait! There was no time for him to slip back into his shoes, and he ran onto the field stocking-footed. This *foot-soldier* was unprepared for the moment he had so desperately desired (see Jeffrey R. Holland, "Bind on Thy Sandals," *Improvement Era*, Sept. 1969, 44).

The dismal experience of this hapless football player should give greater meaning to the importance of *always* remaining ready. Like the five foolish virgins who did not have sufficient oil for the *entire wait*, this young man suffered the consequences of his foolishness (see Matthew 25:1–13).

Consider these words of the Savior: "Wherefore, lift up your hearts and rejoice, and gird up your loins, and take upon you my whole armor, that ye may be able to withstand the evil day, *having done all, that ye may be able to stand.*

"Stand, therefore, having your loins girt about with truth, having on the breastplate of righteousness, *and your feet shod with the preparation of the gospel* of peace" (D&C 27:15–16; emphasis added).

Contrast the experience of the stocking-footed football player with that of Fred, the basketball benchwarmer. Fred had played sparingly throughout the season and had sat on the bench the entire championship game. His team was behind by one point; the other team had the ball and there were only three seconds left in the game.

It was at this critical moment that the coach turned to

Fred and said, "Fred, get in there. I want you to do just one thing, *get the ball!*" Fred's heart sank. He knew he had trained; he had gone through wind sprints; he had been completely obedient to training rules and been to every practice. Yet there were only seconds left, and he had not yet played during the entire game.

He was, however, one who had *stood by ready.* "So when the coach said, 'Sprint, Fred. Get the ball, Fred,' he was so used to being obedient that he just did it. He didn't care about what had happened the rest of the game. It had been worth everything he had prepared for just for those last three seconds."

When play resumed and the ball was inbounded, Fred was ready. He did exactly what he had been asked to do. He got the ball and quickly threw it to his teammate, who scored the winning basket (Rex D. Pinegar, "Be a Winner," address at Salt Lake Institute of Religion, Jan. 22, 1976, 6).

What if Fred, like the discouraged football player, had given up and taken off his shoes?

None of us can afford to be unprepared for defining moments. Nor can any afford to become discouraged because of not being called into immediate action on the front line. Proper preparation and enduring well are as important to future action as the actual moment when we are called on to put into effect the principles practiced and learned.

Several years ago a disastrous flood roared through the quiet community of Rexburg, Idaho. The devastating waters from the breached Teton Dam annihilated the homes, property, and personal possessions of many.

One of those so adversely affected by the raging waters

was a woman who had faithfully adhered to the counsel of the Church to keep a year's supply of food and clothing in her home. As she later viewed the devastation that represented what once were her prized possessions, she was chided by an insensitive acquaintance. "What good did that year's supply do you?" said the skeptic. In response, the faithful Saint said, "I wasn't told that I would ever have to *use* it. I was only told to have it!"

What a masterful discourse on obedience. In spite of her loss, she was an honorable soldier of faith who stood by her principles.

We may not always understand why we are asked to make certain preparations in our lives or why we should avoid certain things that might weaken us physically or spiritually. But incomplete understanding of a principle does not preclude our practicing it, nor our receiving the promised blessings. Obedience is always a wise course.

Occasionally faithful soldiers stand by far from the scene of the action. Yet their impact can be just as meaningful as those who are more visible.

During the epochal flight of Apollo 11 to the moon, astronauts Neil Armstrong and Buzz Aldrin were in the lunar module, Eagle, descending toward man's historic first landing on the moon. As the module rapidly descended toward the lunar surface, the two astronauts suddenly reported a program alarm in the module's computer. It threatened to recycle itself, which would begin all the calculations anew and force Armstrong to abort the mission.

Far from the scene of this drama, a twenty-seven-year-old engineer, Stephen G. Bales, responded as a soldier who *stood by ready* to act. Sitting at the guidance officer's console in Mission Control, he effectively analyzed the problem. His suggested solution was quickly relayed to the floundering module, where it was put into effect and the problem solved. The flight of Eagle resumed, and astronaut Armstrong became the first mortal man to take a historic walk on the dusty surface of the moon—all because a relatively young, unknown engineer stood ready at his post about 240,000 miles away on earth (see "One Small Step—One Giant Leap, The Flight of Apollo 11," *Reader's Digest,* Oct. 1969, 280; excerpted from *Newsweek*).

All of us should be as soldiers who stand by, assuring the safety of others. Most of us will never have the opportunity to effect as dramatic a rescue of an endangered mission as that just described in the flight of Apollo 11. Few will face the task of rushing into a burning building to save others from perishing in flames or smoke, or of performing some other daring deed of physical courage.

All, however, will have opportunities to save others from aborting their spiritual missions here on earth. Many short-circuit the *measure of their creation* because of shortsightedness on their part and because they stood alone during critical moments; they did not have faithful friends who stood by ready to render the necessary assistance.

Elder Robert L. Backman told the story of one young man who had become inactive in the Church, but who, through the persuasive techniques of four of his friends, had agreed to attend a youth conference. The event turned

into a spiritual feast for the faith-famished boy. He joined
his friends in a pact, in which each pledged to the others
that he would live a righteous life. Because friends lifted
him in a moment that mattered, this once inactive boy
turned his life around and accepted a call to serve a mission (see Conference Report, Oct. 1980, 59).

What might have been the fate of Alma the younger
and his wayward companions, the sons of Mosiah, if others had not "prayed with much faith" in their behalf?
(Mosiah 27:14). Should not our prayers similarly be raised
to our Heavenly Father in behalf of the weak and
wayward?

Not many years ago a new stake president was sustained during a conference session conducted by a General
Authority. On that occasion "there were many who were
proud and happy concerning him; but most proud and
most happy was a little man who sat at the stake clerk's
table, a rural mail carrier by profession. He it was who,
twelve years [before], had in quiet, patient labor persuaded
his totally inactive neighbor to come back into activity. It
would have been so much easier to have let that indiffer-
ent neighbor go his own way, and it would have been so
much easier for the mail carrier to have lived his own quiet
life. But he had put aside his personal interests in the interest of another; and that other . . . became the honored and
respected leader of a great stake of Zion" (Gordon B.
Hinckley, "Forget Yourself," *1977 Devotional Speeches of the
Year* [Provo: BYU Press, 1978], 44).

Consider the counsel of the Lord that we should stand

by ready to "succor the weak, lift up the hands which hang down, and strengthen the feeble knees" (D&C 81:5).

Every day we have opportunities to lift, strengthen, and assist others. May we all be as ready as "the soldier who stood by."

Chapter 4

LOST
OPPORTUNITIES

◆ ◆ ◆ ◆ ◆ ◆ ◆ ◆ ◆ ◆

"Then cometh Jesus . . . unto a place called Gethsemane" (Matthew 26:36).

"And being in an agony he prayed more earnestly: and his sweat was as it were great drops of blood falling down to the ground" (Luke 22:44).

"Which suffering caused myself, [Jesus Christ], the greatest of all, to tremble because of pain, and to bleed at every pore, and to suffer both body and spirit—and would that I might not drink the bitter cup, and shrink—nevertheless, glory be to the Father, and I partook and finished my preparations unto the children of men" (D&C 19:18–19).

What if the Savior had decided that the ordeal of Gethsemane was too much for Him to endure? That the pain was too excruciating a price to pay for redeeming us from our sins?

What if Jesus had turned away from Calvary and said, "Gethsemane was sufficient! I am too tired and too pained to suffer any more. Get someone else to finish this job. I have put in my time."

"O the wisdom of God, his mercy and grace! For behold, if the flesh should rise no more our spirits must become subject to that angel who fell from before the presence of the Eternal God, and became the devil, to rise no more. And our spirits must have become like unto him, and we become devils, angels to a devil, to be shut out from the presence of our God, and to remain with the father of lies, in misery, like unto himself" (2 Nephi 9:8–9).

Fortunately for us, the Perfect One did not falter or fail in His divine mission for mankind. He has provided a pattern for us to follow in all things. When we are faced with difficulties or temptations, when we become discouraged or think that we are too tired to carry on, or that we have already sacrificed enough, we can contemplate the Savior's experiences and take courage and strength from Him.

There are many hinge points in history when people were faced with decisions that, wrongly made, would have adversely altered their destiny as well as that of others. Even such a seemingly simple decision as where you should work can have far-reaching consequences.

Shortly after the turn of the century, a returned missionary was seeking employment. He had received a financially attractive offer from the government, which was looking for an individual of sound character to work as an inspector of places that sold beer and liquor and as a collector of excise taxes. The missionary mulled the offer over in his mind and made a tentative decision not to take the job because of the nature of the places he would be required to visit. However, he needed employment and decided to counsel with his father on the matter. The father confirmed the son's decision to decline the offer and wisely said, "Remember this, Son, the best of company is none too good for you." Several days later the returned missionary received an offer to work in the Church

Historian's Office. His acceptance of this job led to a life-long association with that office, where he served for half a century as the historian of The Church of Jesus Christ of Latter-day Saints.

This man also lived to serve sixty years as a member of the Quorum of the Twelve Apostles and to become the tenth president of the Church. The impact of his masterful discourses and writings will be felt for many years to come. Joseph Fielding Smith's "choice of jobs was one of the most important decisions of his life." How different might his life, and the lives of those he touched, have been had he not made the right choice in a moment that mattered! (see Joseph Fielding Smith, Jr., and John J. Stewart, *The Life of Joseph Fielding Smith* [Salt Lake City: Deseret Book, 1972], 125–26).

When courageous, correct action is taken, the rippling effect for good is like that of concentric circles spreading in ever-widening rings of righteousness.

The Book of Mormon relates the story of a marvelous man named Helaman, who led a choice contingent of young men in their fight for freedom. They had been fleeing for more than two days before a powerful army of their enemies. On the third day, Helaman discovered that his young men were no longer being pursued. At this point they faced a critical choice. They knew that their friend Antipus and his soldiers had probably overtaken the enemy army and were engaged in fierce fighting. Antipus and his men were outnumbered and faced certain death if Helaman and his "little sons" (Alma 56:39) did not return to help them.

Although inexperienced in fighting and exhausted from their long march, the young men displayed their courage and faith in God by voting to return and aid Antipus and his beleaguered men.

Helaman records the significance of this decision in these words: "The army of Antipus being weary, because of their long march in so short a space of time, were about to fall into the hands of the Lamanites; and *had I not returned* . . . they would have obtained their purpose" (Alma 56:50; emphasis added).

What if Helaman had not returned? Not only would many lives have been lost, but the liberty of his entire people would have been in peril. Many innocent people, far from the scene of the actual fighting, might have suffered severely if Helaman and his stripling warriors had taken the easy way out and not returned to help the embattled Antipus.

Many opportunities for doing good are lost because some think only of their own comfort and well-being. They tire, get discouraged, or quit because they think they have "put in their time."

Not all defining moments may appear to affect anyone but the one making the decisive decision. Nevertheless, every choice we make has an effect on others beyond ourselves. If I fail to make a proper choice in a moment that matters, am I not adversely affecting my ancestors, their name and lineage, as well as my own real and potential posterity?

When faced with alternative courses of action, we should always look beyond ourselves and ask how the decision will affect our family and friends—past, present, and future—as well as the world in general. No decision regarding our behavior is self-contained; it sets in motion a rippling effect that touches many lives—seen and unseen.

Anciently many families had coats of arms, or family crests, that were proudly passed on to posterity. These crests were symbolic of values the families possessed, and those to whom they were given were expected to honor them through their personal conduct.

Precious heirlooms such as rings and other pieces of jewelry are often passed on from parents to children. The sentimental and emotional value of such heirlooms usually exceeds their monetary value. They are treasured not because of their worth in dollars, but because they represent a tangible tie to departed loved ones.

Although not all of us have family crests or precious heirlooms that have been passed on from concerned and caring ancestors, each of us possesses a *royal* birthright. As children of our Father in Heaven, we are heirs to royal crowns of righteousness in the realms of the hereafter (see D&C 29:13). Our choices and actions will determine whether we receive or forfeit our heavenly heritage. In this respect, we would do well to heed the counsel of the Lord: "Hold that fast which thou hast, that no man take thy crown" (Revelation 3:11).

Unfortunately, some forget the promised crown and do not always respond righteously when faced with critical choices. Some years ago a group of four Latter-day Saint boys set out on a cross-country trip following their high school graduation. This was their first experience in being away from the direct influence of their parents, and they decided to try some of the forbidden fruits of the world.

One boy said that they could afford to "let their hair down" and just sample sin. "What difference will it make?" he said. "Nobody out here in the world knows us or cares anything about our church connections."

Later that day they sat in a bar of a distant city, each with a mug of beer, pretending to enjoy the beverage, which satisfied neither their physical taste buds nor their spiritual thirst.

Suddenly a stranger came into the bar and, with a deliberate pace, walked straight to their table. He extended his hand to one of the boys and said, "I beg your pardon, but aren't you George Redford's son from Utah?" Panic stricken, the young man confessed that he was. "I thought I recognized you," continued the stranger. "I'm Henry Paulsen, vice-president of the company your dad works for, and I met you and your mother last winter at a company dinner at the Hotel Utah. I have never forgotten how you explained your Mormon priesthood to one of the other executives of our company who asked you what it meant to be a Mormon boy. I must say I was a little surprised to see you head for the bar, but I suppose that with Mormons as well as non-Mormons, boys will be boys when they're off the roost" (see Marion G. Romney, "Integrity," *Ensign*, Nov. 1974, 73–74).

"And there shall also be many which shall say: Eat, drink, and be merry; nevertheless, fear God—he will justify in committing a *little* sin" (2 Nephi 28:8; emphasis added).

"And thus the devil cheateth their souls, and leadeth them away carefully down to hell" (2 Nephi 28:21).

What if those young men had held to their principles? What impact might it have made upon the executive of the company for which one boy's father worked? Could the damage of this experience ever be erased?

Contrast this experience with that of the examples set by other young people who were likewise observed by one not of their faith. An individual from Minnesota wrote to Brigham Young University to describe his experience on a bus trip through parts of the Midwest and South:

"There was a large group of young men and women traveling. . . . These fine young people were students from Brigham Young [University] going home for the holidays.

"They were all very polite, well-behaved, articulate young men and women. It was a pleasure to travel with them—to know them—and it gave me a new hope for the future" (see Thomas S. Monson, "Profiles of Faith," *Ensign,* Nov. 1978, 55).

What if this contingent of young Latter-day Saints had been letting their hair down and sampling forbidden fruits of the world?

Another young Latter-day Saint showed his courage under great social pressure. He had gone away to an officers' training school where he was expected to conform to the standards and customs of the group. A new commanding officer arrived, and a banquet was prepared to honor him. By every plate was a cocktail glass, filled with an alcoholic beverage, which was to be used to toast the new commanding officer. At the appointed time, all cadets but one raised their cocktail glasses in honor of their new chief. The one exception was the Latter-day Saint who stood conspicuously alone with his toast. It was a glass of *milk!*

His unique toast did not go unnoticed by the new commander, who later asked the cadet why he had toasted him with milk. "Well, sir," he said, "I've never touched alcohol in my life. I don't want to touch it; my parents wouldn't want me to touch it; and I didn't think you would want me to either. I wanted to toast you, so I thought you would be satisfied if I toasted you with what I am accustomed to drinking."

The young man was asked to report to the commander's office in the morning, and he spent a sleepless night wondering if his career was through. This uncertainty did not change his thinking about the action he had taken, however, for he knew it was right.

In the morning he was pleasantly surprised to find the commander assigning him a place on his personal staff with this explanation: "I want to surround myself with men who have the courage to do what they think is right regardless of what anybody else thinks about it" (N. Eldon Tanner, "Are You Taking Your Priesthood for Granted?" *Ensign*, May 1976, 43–44).

What opportunities might have been lost had this young man not had the courage to hold to his principles in a moment that mattered?

"Boy, 16, Dies: Alcohol Blamed."

This tragic headline appeared in a newspaper a few years ago. The story related how a high school student had attended a party where he had consumed more than half a gallon of hard liquor before he passed out. He was placed on a couch to sleep off the effects of his drunken stupor but never awakened. The ultimate tragedy of this untimely death was that the young victim was a member of The Church of Jesus Christ of Latter-day Saints, which clearly teaches total abstinence from such harmful substances as alcohol.

What if he had held to the principles taught by the Church to which he belonged?

Another young Latter-day Saint faced a defining moment. He was the only child of a family that lived on a ranch fourteen miles away from their chapel. One Saturday night he received a phone call from a friend who invited him to go on a snowmobiling excursion the next morning. The boy asked his mother if he could go.

This wise woman left the decision to the boy, with this gentle prod: "Son, you're twelve years old," she said. "You hold the priesthood of God. You can make up your own mind about that."

The boy had the courage to make the correct choice and declined the invitation from his friend. The next morning as he and his parents were walking into the chapel for their worship services, they saw a truck go by with those who were going on the snowmobiling trip. As the truck passed them, this faithful deacon said, "Gee, I wish I could have convinced my friends that they should be in priesthood this morning."

How significant was this boy's decision to choose correctly, for that Sunday would be his last opportunity to honor the Sabbath in his mortal life. He was killed in a farm accident later that same week (see Marion D. Hanks, Melbourne Area Conference Report, Feb. 27–29, 1976, 33).

Contemplate how grateful this young man was that he had so recently made the right choice in a mortal moment that mattered. What if he had gone snowmobiling? How different might his reunion with his loved ones have been when he passed through the veil that separates the spirit world from mortality?

Contrast the courage of this young man to stand up for what was right to the near-tragic experience of a man who just once made the wrong decision regarding keeping the Sabbath holy.

Elder William Grant Bangerter tells the story: "I have a friend who one time went on a family outing to Yellowstone Park. While he was faithful to his commitments as a member and leader in the Church, some of his relatives tended to scoff at his 'strait-laced' religious nature. They persuaded him, one Sunday morning, to go out in the boat fishing with them. Suddenly a strong wind arose, and they found themselves in such danger that they feared for their lives. The taunting and skepticism were suddenly gone. In plaintive unison they looked to my friend, saying, 'Please, can't you pray for us?' They evidently had little confidence in their own petitions or perhaps sensed their unworthiness to call for divine aid. The irony of the situation is that my friend, having been tempted against his better judgment to do something of which he felt the Lord would not approve, says of his predicament: 'I had no prayer to offer. All I could think of was the headline in the newspaper saying, "Stake President Drowns While Fishing on Sunday"'" (Conference Report, Oct. 1979, 13).

Happily for this man and his friends, they did get back safely. What if the boat had capsized and he had drowned? How would he have felt in meeting our Father in Heaven and the Savior? How would those who trusted him as their leader have felt? No one can afford to let his or her standards down even once.

Occasionally lost opportunities come because of our unwillingness to respond to a call for help or service. Consider the case of the man whose choice in a moment that mattered deprived him of a promised blessing.

An inspired patriarch had promised him that one day he would have the opportunity to preside over a stake of Zion. Yet, when the call came, it was inconvenient for him to serve at that particular time, and he declined. He asked that the Brethren give him time to take care of some pressing business matters and that he would be happy to serve sometime in the future. The call was never reissued. The door to the fulfillment of that promised opportunity was forever padlocked (see Harold Glen Clark, "I Know Not, Save the Lord Commanded Me," *Devotional Speeches of the Year* [Provo: BYU Press, 1973], 17–18).

Contrast the above experience with that of another who was call to serve at an inconvenient time in his life. His call to serve as a stake president in Japan was a severe sacrifice, for he had just accepted a promotion in his company that necessitated his moving to another city. His old job had already been promised to another man, and his company was just waiting for him to move. The General

Authority conducting the interview, a member of the Quorum of the Twelve Apostles, asked the man to lay his promotion on the altar of sacrifice. He was asked to approach his employer and request that he not be transferred but that he remain in his present location so he could accept the call to serve as stake president.

Although he was reluctant to turn down his promotion, the man was obedient to the counsel and called his employer with what must have seemed a strange request. The company president asked the man to reconsider and gave him five minutes to think about it before calling him back with a final decision. "In that short interval of time, he would be forced to make a decision that would affect the rest of his life."

The troubled man called Elder Adney Y. Komatsu, a General Authority who was supervising the work of the Church in Japan, to seek counsel. Elder Komatsu said:

"My reply to him was that the Lord had sent one of his Apostles to organize a stake in Zion in Japan. If he had to give his answer to the Lord himself, would it be any different? He thanked me, then called his employer.

"Early the next morning, he came to the mission home and was officially called as the new stake president. When the General Authority inquired about his status with the company, the [man] responded that his promotion was canceled and that he would have to accept whatever they decided to give him.

"Before he left, the General Authority blessed this man and stated that although he would go through a period of trials and tribulations at work, the time would come when he would be called upon by his employer to help make great and important decisions for his company, because he had made a decision to serve the Lord rather than to accept personal gain.

"A few years later, this man—still a stake president—became the assistant to the president of his company, fulfilling the promise made by an Apostle of the Lord" (Conference Report, Oct. 1979, 100).

What if he had thought the initial sacrifice too great and had turned down the opportunity to serve?

Not many years ago a young lawyer was immersed in pursuing his career with a law firm in Chicago. He was working six days a week, morning, noon, and night, on some challenging legal problems. One day he received a phone call from his stake president, who invited him to lunch. The president issued a stake mission call to the already overworked lawyer and told him that he would be expected to give forty hours a month in proselyting time in addition to attending meetings, bringing investigators to Church, and pursuing an individual gospel study program.

The young lawyer must have wondered where he could find that extra forty hours of time, but in a moment that mattered he mustered the necessary faith to accept the call. With faith similar to that of Nephi (see 1 Nephi 3:7), the man responded, "If the Lord wants me to serve in that position—and I do honor the calling as coming from the Lord through his servant—he will make it possible for me to do it. When do you want me to start?"

The president, who was also acting on faith, said, "I have an appointment I'd like you to keep tonight."

The lawyer's name was Dallin H. Oaks, a man who would later be called to serve as president of Brigham Young University and who now serves as a member of the Quorum of the Twelve Apostles. What if he had said no to the call to sacrifice and serve as a stake missionary? Would these other opportunities ever have been his?

As he later reflected on this moment that mattered in his life, Elder Oaks said, "This was a turning point in my life; this was a test of my faith.

"That calling . . . offered me an opportunity to grow in faith and devotion and loyalty to the leadership of the Church. In every way I can measure it was a turning point in my life" ("The Blessing of Commandments," *Speeches of the Year, 1974* [Provo: BYU Press, 1975], 224–25).

Occasionally opportunities for achieving success come in quiet, almost unnoticed ways. Success is often the result of one's ability to put forth his best effort regardless of how trivial, boring, or repetitive a task may be.

Years ago a struggling young actor named Pat O'Brien had a part in a play that was receiving less than favorable reviews. The show had already been moved to a smaller theater, and the actors had taken a salary cut. O'Brien had one scene that was particularly demanding of his talents and his emotional reserves. "Many nights I was tempted just to coast through this difficult scene," he said. "*After all,* I thought, *why knock yourself out on something with no future.*

"But, somehow, a Bible verse from my catechism days echoed in my memory. 'Whatever task lies to your hand, do it with all your might' (Ecclesiastes 9:10).

"And so at every performance I still put my all into

that scene, and wound up wringing wet from the effort and sometimes feeling foolish."

Unknown to the actor, a film director was in the audience one night and was so impressed with O'Brien's efforts that the actor was later given an important part in one of the director's movies. That was the start of a successful film career for Pat O'Brien (excerpted with permission from *Guideposts* magazine. Copyright © 1982 by Guideposts Associates, Inc., Carmel, New York 10512).

What if he had not given his all to that demanding scene in the less than successful stage show? What if he had not done his best on just that *one* night when the film director was present?

Sometimes people give up on a goal because they have been battered by obstacles placed in their path. They tire of constantly having their emotional shins bruised by stumbling blocks. It is so much easier to relax and rest rather than to relentlessly pursue a blocked goal. The names of those who give up their quest for excellence will not be mentioned when deeds of courage are spoken by their fellowmen. On the other hand, there will always be those who refuse to surrender to setbacks. On the other hand, there will always be those who refuse to surrender to setbacks. Lance Armstrong is one of these.

As a young boy Lance became enamored with cycling, spending hours on end in riding countless miles on his bicycle. He became a well-known participant in many amateur races and was accustomed to consistently finishing among the winners. In 1992, at the age of nineteen, Lance decided to join the ranks of the professional cyclists.

His first professional effort was in the Classico San Sebastian race in Europe, where he encountered the horrendous weather conditions that often prevail in European races. The soaking wet and physically spent young racer crossed the finish line in last place, twenty-seven minutes behind the winner. Yet this future champion would not be discouraged or deterred from his desire to compete. His motto was, "Despite the odds, don't quit!"

Three years after his failure, Lance became the first American to win first place in the same race in which he had finished last during his professional racing debut. He rose quickly in the ranks of renowned cyclists, winning many races and much acclaim. Then a severe setback took place. In a press conference on October 9, 1996, a stunned public learned that Lance Armstrong was afflicted with testicular cancer that had spread to his lungs and his brain. His chances of survival were less than 50 percent.

Two operations followed within the next several weeks, followed by months of aggressive chemotherapy. Lance simply would not give up. Five months later, against all odds, he once again resumed his cycle training. Just a year and a half after undergoing cancer surgery, Lance Armstrong won the Spirit 56K Criterium race in Austin, Texas. However, later that year he had to drop out of the Paris-Nice race, and it appeared his racing career was over. Yet with determination, and the encouragement of family and friends, he finished the year by winning fourth place in the World Championship race in Holland.

His stunning victory in the prestigious Tour de France race in July of 1999 was unprecedented. The world had a new hero—a man who had not only beaten physical adversity but who now was a role model, a spokesperson giving hope and encouragement to others who have suffered setbacks. As of this writing (2003), Lance Armstrong has now been a winner at the Tour de France on four occasions. "Regardless of one victory, two victories, [or] four victories," he said, "there's never been a victory by a cancer survivor. That's a fact that hopefully I'll be remembered for" (see http://www.lancearmstrong.com).

Another who received encouragement at a discouraging time was a young married man named Rex D. Pinegar. At the age of twenty-three, he found himself a freshman in college. He struggled through two unsuccessful semesters of studies. He finally received a letter informing him that unless he improved his academic status, he would be asked to leave the campus.

At this hinge point in his life, he received loving encouragement from his wife, motivating him to change. He said to himself, "Hey, Rex, wake up. What you do at a university affects your eternal life, not just your life here in the earth. Why? Because you establish habits of learning. You establish an awareness of right and wrong. You establish an awareness of improvement in terms of conditions for living. You establish a relationship with other people which helps you to evaluate yourself in terms of effectiveness with other people and just how influential you can be in changing your own life for the better."

So, he made a decision. Not only would he change, but he would change dramatically. He decided he was going to be on the honor roll the next semester. He prayed about it and then pursued this goal. From then on, through the completion of his doctoral degree, he was always on the honor roll. Because he decided to commit himself to academic excellence, he now has the right to use the title of *Dr.* Rex D. Pinegar. More significantly, however, his commitment to spiritual excellence brought him into the ranks of the General Authorities of The Church of Jesus Christ of Latter-day Saints, where he exchanged his academic title for a more spiritually significant one: *Elder* Rex D. Pinegar (see Rex D. Pinegar, "Our Relationship with Christ," address at the Salt Lake Institute of Religion, Mar. 11. 1977, 6–7).

What if his wife had not encouraged him at a critical moment? What if he had not decided to change? Where might he have been today? How many lives have been blessed because of one man's critical choice in a moment that mattered?

Chapter 5

STUMBLING BLOCKS
OR STEPPING-STONES

❖ ❖ ❖ ❖ ❖ ❖ ❖ ❖ ❖ ❖

"It must needs be, that there is an opposition in all things," declared the prophet Lehi (2 Nephi 2:11). A more modern version of that declaration is found in the words of a song that was popular in my youth: "Into each life some rain must fall!"

Such "rain" or opposition often causes one to murmur and to complain that life is not fair. Elder Neal A. Maxwell observed, "A basic cause of murmuring is that too many of us seem to expect that life will flow ever smoothly, featuring an unbroken chain of green lights with empty parking places just in front of our destinations!" (*Ensign*, Nov. 1989, 82).

When we face obstacles and opposition in our lives, we are faced with a choice. We may see such times as stepping-stones to growth—learning and strengthening experiences—or we may see them as stumbling blocks, begin to murmur, and simply give up. Our attitude on such occasions will determine our degree of happiness both now and in the future.

Consider the circumstances of Elder Henry B. Eyring's paternal grandmother. She faced a significant moment that mattered when her doctor informed her that she had incurable stomach cancer. Faced with the certainty of suffering and death, she chose to make the most of her remaining time on earth. She chose happiness over gloom.

On the way home from the doctor's office, she said to her teenage son, "Now, Henry, let's be cheerful. Let's sing hymns." And so a duet of singing began that included "O My Father" (*Hymns,* no. 292) and "Come, Come, Ye Saints" (*Hymns,* no. 30). The latter hymn includes such declarations of faith as "no toil nor labor fear; / But with joy wend your way;" "Why should we mourn or think our lot is hard? / 'Tis not so; all is right;" "Gird up your loins; fresh courage take. / Our God will never us forsake;" "We'll make the air with music ring, / Shout praises to our God and King;" "And should we die before our journey's through, / Happy day! All is well!"

What a legacy of faith that grandmother left her posterity in that defining moment! Said her grandson Elder Eyring, "When tragedy strikes or even when it looms, our families will have the opportunity to look into our hearts to see whether we know what we said we knew. Our children will watch, feel the Spirit confirm that we lived as we preached, remember that confirmation, and pass the story across the generations" (*Ensign,* May 1996, 64).

Another who lifted others while suffering severely was a woman who was known for her ebullient spirit and constant smile. "You are such a joy to all of us," said a friend and admirer. "What is your secret? Can you tell me?"

The surprising response came in one word. "Malignant!" replied the woman. She then went on to explain to her friend that when her doctor told her of her condition, she concluded she had a choice to make. "I could make everyone miserable or I could try to make others happy" she said. "On my knees I realized that I had one day at a time just as everyone else has. I was able to see things I had never seen. My husband, my children, each person took on a beauty you can't believe. I know that life is a gift whether it be a day or a year and I intend to enjoy my gift to the maximum" (*Ensign*, May 1979, 67).

Occasionally adversity comes in the form of a failure on the sports field, in the classroom, in a relationship, or in some other endeavor upon which we have set our hopes. Our reactions on such occasions become pivotal points in determining our future happiness and success in other arenas of life.

Abraham Lincoln is a name recognized and honored by millions as a successful leader. Yet, in spite of his renown and ultimate success, his early life was full of failure. In his first try at political office, running for the Illinois state legislature, he was badly beaten. His first attempt in business failed, and he spent the next seventeen years of his life paying off debts. He fell in love and became engaged to a beautiful woman who died before they were married. Additional efforts in seeking political office were met with defeat as he ran unsuccessfully for both the U.S. House of Representatives and the Senate. Yet he picked himself up after each failure and moved ahead toward his destiny. What might the American people have lost had President Abraham Lincoln not guided this nation through the terrible conflict of the Civil War?

Another esteemed United States president was Harry S. Truman. Thrust into the presidency during critical days of

World War II, President Truman earned a place in history through his strong though often controversial leadership. Following his retirement from the presidency, he was one day visiting the presidential library named in his honor when he engaged some young school children in conversation. "Was you popular when you was a boy?" asked one child. "Why no," replied the former president, "I was never popular." He went on to say that the popular boys seemed to be the ones who were good at games. "Without my glasses," he said, "I was blind as a bat, and to tell the truth, I was kind of a sissy" (*Vital Speeches of the Day*, Feb. 1983, 6).

Certainly any who ever stood nose to nose with President Harry S. Truman never considered him to be a sissy!

Physical or intellectual impairments don't need to deter one from enjoying life to its fullest. Some years ago, a representative of The Church of Jesus Christ of Latter-day Saints was visiting in one of the developing countries of the world in an effort to improve living conditions there. An appreciative teenage boy asked if the visitor would take a gift back to the president of the Church at that time, Spencer W. Kimball. The gift was a sketch the boy had drawn of a peacock with its tail feathers in full fan. It was a masterpiece of patient and creative effort, with each colorful feather in just the right place.

When the gift was presented to this great leader, President Kimball marveled at the picture's beauty and the pinpoint detail with which it had been drawn. Then he was handed a photograph of the young artist. He was shocked to see the lad had no arms. The intricate drawing had been created as the handicapped artist held his pencils between his toes (*Ensign*, Nov. 1977, 82).

At the age of five Shelly Mann was stricken with the dreaded disease of polio. When it was through ravaging her little body, the child was left without use of her arms or her legs. Undaunted, Shelly began daily therapy in a swimming pool, where it was hoped the buoyancy of the water would help lift her almost lifeless limbs as she struggled to gain their use once again.

Her untiring efforts paid off as little by little, virtually inch by inch, she slowly gained the ability to lift an arm out of the water and then to stand unassisted in the pool. Then came the next goal—to swim the width of the pool. Then came the goal of swimming the length of the pool, followed by several lengths.

Patience, persistence, and undoubtedly some pain transformed Shelly from a helpless little girl to a world-champion athlete. At the 1960 Olympics in Melbourne, Australia, Shelly Mann stood on the pinnacle of the platform of athletic excellence as she received the gold medal for her performance in the butterfly swimming stroke.

In spite of one's best efforts, gold medals and blue ribbons are not always achieved. But the important thing is what an individual does with the talents or resources he or she possesses.

John Helander is a native of Sweden who refused to let a physical handicap deter him from participating in events where he was clearly at a disadvantage. His motor skills don't function normally, and it is difficult for him to coordinate his bodily motions.

At a youth conference in Kungsbacka, Sweden, John took part in a 1,500-meter running race. He had no chance of winning a medal, but he was determined to win his *own* race—a competition with endurance and doing *his* best.

The young man was not even halfway around the first lap when runners were passing him on their second lap. Finally, the winner passed the finish line and broke the tape to the cheers of the crowd. The other contestants soon crossed the finish line, and the race was over. Or was it?

There in the distance was a lone, struggling runner. As he finally crossed the finish line he kept running, for this was only his first completed lap, with another yet to go. The crowd remained in their seats, eyes fixed on this image of courage on the racetrack. When John Helander finally approached the finish line, the crowd rose to its feet and happily cheered him on. The officials at the finish line even fixed a new tape across the track, which the exhausted runner broke as he stumbled across the line to his own victory (*Ensign*, May 1987, 69).

Sometimes circumstances beyond our control work against even our best efforts to cross the finish line. In such moments, it is attitude that matters so very much.

Cliff Cushman, as a member of the United States Olympic team, won the silver medal in the 400-meter hurdles during the 1960 competition. He seemed to be a prime candidate for the gold medal four years later. In an unfortunate slip during the American trials, he made a misstep and tripped. There was no second chance, no opportunity to run the race again. This singular mistake eliminated Cliff from the team. In an instant his dream was shattered.

Well-wishers flooded his home with messages of sympathy. Yet Cliff Cushman was not one to wallow in self-pity. He was determined that a moment of defeat not be turned into a life of defeat. In an open letter to the youth of his hometown, Grand Forks, North Dakota, he wrote, "Over 15 years ago, I saw a star—first place in the Olympic Games. I literally started to run after it. In 1960 I came within three yards of grabbing it; this year I stumbled, fell and watched it recede four more years away. . . .

"In a split second all the many years of training, pain, sweat, blisters and agony of running were simply and irrevocably wiped out.

"But I tried! I would much rather fail knowing I had put forth an honest effort than never to have tried at all. . . .

"Certainly I was very disappointed in falling flat on my face. However, there is nothing I can do about it now but get up, pick the cinders from my wounds, and take one more step followed by one more and one more, until the steps turn into miles and miles into success.

"I know I may never make it. The odds are against me, but I have something in my favor—desire and faith. . . . At least I am going to try. How about you? . . . Unless your reach exceeds your grasp, how can you be sure what you can attain? . . .

"Let me tell you something about yourselves. . . . You

are spending more money, enjoying more freedom, and driving more cars than ever before, yet many of you are very unhappy. Some of you have never known the satisfaction of doing your best in sports, the joy of excelling in class, the wonderful feeling of completing a job, any job, and looking back on it knowing that you have done your best. . . .

"I dare you to look up at the stars, not down at the mud, and set your sights on them that, up to now, you thought were unattainable. There is plenty of room at the top, but no room for anyone to sit down.

"Who knows? You may be surprised at what you can achieve with sincere effort. So get up, pick the cinders out of your wounds, and take one more step.

"I dare you!" (see *Ensign*, Nov. 1976, 30–31).

Most of us will never stand in the winner's circle, hear the roar of the crowd applauding our feats, or see our name headlined in the news media. However, to know that we have *done* our best and *been* our best regardless of the circumstances is what really matters. Fame is fleeting. It is character that counts!

You never fail until you quit trying. All stumbling blocks can ultimately become stepping-stones, opening new doors and creating new horizons. In defining moments believe in your best self and act with faith upon that belief.

Baseball's all-time home-run hitter, Hank Aaron, never would have achieved his feat had he succumbed to self-pity and a feeling of defeat when his minor-league manager described him as unable to play the game. And what about the famous poet Robert Frost? As a struggling young poet, his work was rejected by the poetry editor for the *Atlantic Monthly* as unacceptable for publication. Or consider the great British statesman and world leader Sir Winston Churchill, known for his stirring speeches. As a sixteen-year-old schoolboy he received a low evaluation from his rhetoric teacher, who said the lad's speaking efforts were "a conspicuous lack of success."

Perhaps an occasional bump in the road, a stumbling block, a temporary setback might turn out to be a wake-up call, a much-needed reality check that we can be and do better. As a teenager, Neal A. Maxwell received a D- from his English teacher, the first low grade he had ever received. "The shock treatment worked," he later wrote. "Challenged by [the teacher's] demands for better performance—which both she and I knew was a realistic requirement—a modest adventure with words and writing really began. There were better grades and better days because the integrity of her scholarship would not accept anything less than the best possible. Her insistence reached me as conveying not simply a dry, antiseptic concern with scholarship, but a concern for me and my potential which said in the form of a compliment, 'You can do better!'" (*A More Excellent Way* [Salt Lake City: Deseret Book, 1967], 134).

Because a teacher cared, a young mind was awakened to its potential, and the Church and the world have been greatly blessed by the writings, wisdom, and eloquent oratory of Elder Neal A. Maxwell of the Quorum of the Twelve Apostles.

A budding author named Theodor Seuss Geisel had

his first manuscript rejected by more than forty publishers before it was finally accepted. Thus began a writing career that lasted decades and produced millions of copies of books that have delighted children and adults alike who have followed the antics of the characters and words created by the man the world knows as "Dr. Seuss."

Failure need not be final!

The renowned author Og Mandino wrote, "If we lock ourselves in a prison of failure and self-pity, we are the only jailers . . . we have the only key to our freedom" (*The Greatest Miracle in the World* [Hollywood, Fla.: Frederick Fell Publishers, 1975], 61).

And President Gordon B. Hinckley said, "There is no obstacle too great, no challenge too difficult, that we cannot meet with faith" (*Ensign*, Nov. 1983, 53).

Chapter 6

MAKING MATTERS
BETTER

♦ ♦ ♦ ♦ ♦ ♦ ♦ ♦ ♦ ♦

"To make matters worse" are words most people have heard. The statement seems to be a connecting phrase between at least two parts of a woeful tale of misfortune. Something bad has happened and then—*to make matters worse*—it is followed by further difficulty that is often more disruptive or damaging than the first encounter of bad fortune.

The way we respond to misfortune can determine the depth of the disruption, disappointment, or damage. To throw up our hands and give up in despair, or to react in some foolish, knee-jerk fashion will certainly "make matters worse."

A skilled and renowned surgeon received a phone call one night from a fellow physician who pled for assistance. He was operating on a young child and had run into some complications. Could the surgeon please come immediately to the hospital to help save the child's life? The response was quick, and the surgeon was soon on his way across town to the hospital. However, as he pulled up to a stop sign, a man in a brown leather jacket suddenly opened the door, and pretending to have a gun in his pocket, forced the surgeon from his car and drove off, leaving the doctor stranded on the roadside.

Some time later the surgeon was finally able to get to

the hospital, but it was too late. The child had died just moments before. How tragic! Had the man in the brown leather jacket not interrupted the doctor's errand of mercy, the child might have been saved. The attending physician asked the surgeon to accompany him to relay the news to the grieving parents. As the two doctors entered the privacy of the waiting room, the surgeon suddenly gasped, for the sorrowing father was the man in the brown leather jacket. In a moment that mattered very much, the panicked father had taken a course of action that actually increased his suffering and sorrow.

When confronted with difficulties, our challenge is to respond in a wise and prayerful way that makes matters better rather than allowing panic or pity to make matters worse.

Diane was captain of the University of Utah's first national women's championship gymnastics team. Her years of sacrifice, discipline, and training had paid off, and she seemed to be on the pinnacle of success. Then the unthinkable happened. A slight miscalculation of a body rotation she was doing caused her to land on her neck, damaging her spinal cord and resulting in paralysis from the chest down.

Faced with a choice of withdrawing in self-pity, living on past dreams, or moving forward and making the most of her circumstances, Diane courageously and wisely chose the latter course. Two and a half years after her tragic accident, she graduated from the university. During those years on campus Diane was a familiar sight in her wheelchair, with her ever-present smile of hope and genuine cheerfulness making a difference in the lives of others as well as herself. Her handicap allowed others the opportunity to render occasional assistance. "When I came to steep hills," she said, "I made friends in a hurry."

Following her graduation, Diane achieved her goal of becoming a teacher, and her positive attitude has influenced the lives of the children who were fortunate to come under her care. "I'm genuinely happy and content with my life," she declared. "I'm not bitter or angry. In a way I'm just as athletic as I ever was" (*Ensign*, Nov. 1984, 21–22).

Some challenged people are born with limitations that require the patient love and tutoring of others who genuinely care to make matters better. Such was the case with a baby girl born in the Philippines. She came into this world without hands and with only one leg. In less favorable home circumstances, the handicapped child might have been neglected and her potential been undeveloped. Providentially, she was loved and nurtured in a home where she grew to womanhood with self-confidence and faith.

"Despite what to others may have been a *handicap*, to her must have been only a *difficulty*," said one observer of her achievements. She served a full-time proselyting mission for The Church of Jesus Christ of Latter-day Saints and later married and became a mother. Parents, friends, and the woman herself withstood the temptation to make matters worse by blindly limiting her development (*Ensign*, Nov. 1987, 24; emphasis added).

Elder M. Russell Ballard observed, "Some children receive mortal bodies with limitations that might restrict their physical activities but not their spiritual development" (*Ensign*, Nov. 1978, 66). And the Prophet Joseph Smith declared, "All the minds and spirits that God ever sent into the world are susceptible of enlargement" (*Teachings of the Prophet Joseph Smith*, sel. Joseph Fielding Smith [Salt Lake City: Deseret Book, 1938], 354).

On occasion an expectant mother is counseled to abort the child she is carrying because medical tests show it may be born with handicaps or even be incapable of living much beyond birth. Certainly such decisions must be prayerfully pondered. One such situation involved a woman who was told by her physician that her child would unquestionably be born with Down's syndrome; the doctor recommended an abortion.

Now, of a certainty, the loving parents of children who have been born with this limitation would protest, knowing that these special children have brought great happiness into their lives. But let us return to the case at hand. What course of action should this expectant mother and her husband take? There were many voices urging them to follow the advice of one trained and learned in such matters.

In the ultimate sense, only One Voice really mattered! What did Heavenly Father want? What did the Spirit whisper in answer to prayerful supplications?

Personal prayerful pleadings for divine direction were accompanied by an inspired priesthood blessing. Through one of His worthy servants, the Lord promised the woman that the little child within her would be normal and healthy. And so it was! (*Ensign*, Nov. 1989, 80).

What if faith had given way to fear and the woman had submitted to the abortion? How tragic would have been the results! Matters certainly would have been worse!

It should be remembered that not all pre-birth medical diagnoses are wrong. In fact, most are probably right. Yet the question remains, "Should one automatically follow learned counsel, or should one seek the direction of the Spirit?" The answer, which has such far-reaching eternal implications, is obvious: "Follow the Spirit!"

Another example of making matters better by following the Spirit and inspired counsel involved an expectant mother who contracted the dreaded German measles during her pregnancy. Once again the counsel of well-meaning physicians and friends was to abort the normal course of events. Surely, they argued, this child would be severely handicapped if allowed to develop to full term.

The worried woman and her husband counseled with their priesthood leaders—the bishop and stake president. After prayerful consideration, the couple was counseled to put their trust in the Lord and allow this child a chance at life. Except for a hearing loss, the child was born normal and became a joy to her parents and family. She learned to compensate for her slight handicap and upon graduation from high school earned a scholarship to a major university (*Ensign*, May 1985, 12–13).

Speaking of the need to learn to compensate for some perceived or real shortcoming, consider those whose youthful zeal includes dreams of prominence in the athletic arena. So much publicity and acclaim is accorded to sports in our world that many young people see athletic acumen as the elixir that will surely bring them fame and fortune. In fact, a popular phrase recently used by advertisers to promote their products was "I want to be like —————" (a well-known sports figure).

Very few of these "wanna-be's" achieve their dreams of becoming superstars, starters, or even benchwarmers in school or professional sports.

As a young man, Glenn was of small stature but athletic for his size. He decided to try out for the sophomore basketball team at his high school, dreaming of cheerleaders and crowds lavishing him with praise for his game-winning shots. However, when the team list was posted, his name was missing from the roster.

Disappointed but undaunted, he next tried out for the school football team. After all, he reasoned, he was fast and could probably be a star running back. Alas, in the tryouts he was flattened by a rather large lineman. As his aching and limp body was carried off the field, he heard the coach praising the boy who had tackled him with such ferocity.

Now, Glenn could have made matters worse by playing the "woe is me" game, retreating into a world of self-pity. However, he said, "I made a marvelous discovery: there is a lot more to life than sports." He began to look at talents in other fields and developed a new appreciation for classmates who performed in areas other than the sports arena. "A whole new world began to appear," he said. "The disappointment I suffered relative to high school athletics softened my heart and increased my love and appreciation for a broad spectrum of friends at school."

This new perspective led him to excellence in his school studies and to a life of dedicated service in The Church of Jesus Christ of Latter-day Saints. Today he is known as Elder Glenn L. Pace, one of the General Authorities of the Church (*Spiritual Plateaus* [Salt Lake City: Deseret Book, 1991], 79–81).

Of course, few people will ever be called as general officers of the Church. However, success and satisfaction in life do not depend upon prominent positions. The faithful priesthood bearer who quietly goes about his seemingly small but eternally significant assignments can find great joy in such service. Similarly, the young woman or Relief Society sister who reaches out in loving service as a teacher of children or as a compassionate neighbor not only makes a difference for good in the lives of others but receives personal satisfaction from such selfless acts.

A prophet of God has declared, "Your obligation is as serious in your sphere of responsibility as is my obligation in my sphere. No calling in this church is small or of little consequence" (President Gordon B. Hinckley, *Ensign*, May 1995, 71).

One area that challenges one's spiritual and emotional mettle is that of dating, courtship, and marriage. Although the ways of the world have made significant encroachments against the God-given institutions of marriage, home, and family, the standard set by our Father in Heaven remains firm: "Marriage between a man and a woman is ordained of God and . . . the family is central to the Creator's plan for the eternal destiny of His children" ("The Family: A Proclamation to the World," The First

Presidency and Council of the Twelve Apostles of The Church of Jesus Christ of Latter-day Saints).

The challenge is that not all who desire marriage and who have lived worthy of being loved and honored as someone's spouse and eternal companion will receive that great blessing in this life. Consider the case of Sheri Dew. She grew up with the expectation that she would become a wife and mother. Yet as of this writing that blessing has thus far eluded her. People "have no idea how many times I've cried myself to sleep because of acute loneliness or the hundreds of times I've fasted and prayed to be married," she says.

Sheri might have withdrawn and become bitter, making matters worse, but she has chosen the higher road to make matters better for herself and for others. In a momentous moment of inspired self-discovery, she said "I had a very clear impression that I should quit worrying about what I didn't have, because I had plenty, and that I needed to do something with what I'd been given. At that point, my view of the world started very slowly to change."

Discovering and developing her talents, she has become a gifted writer and much-sought-after speaker whose wit and wisdom have inspired millions. She was called to serve as a counselor in the General Relief Society presidency, where her notable service touched lives throughout the world. Upon completing this five-year call, she was made the chief operating officer of Deseret Book Company, where her work of lifting and inspiring others continues ("Living the Unexpected Life," *Deseret News*, March 10, 2002, A1, A7, A11).

Chapter 7

FORGIVENESS: SHEDDING SHACKLES

♦ ♦ ♦ ♦ ♦ ♦ ♦ ♦ ♦ ♦

"Don't let a mistake injure you twice as it does if you harbor a past wrong or injustice and let your anger destroy you" (*Ensign*, May 1982, 12). This simple but significant truth spoken by the late Elder Hugh W. Pinnock, if taken to heart, would soothe the suffering of so many who have suffered needlessly because of their unwillingness to forgive the mistakes of others.

Over a period of years while serving in Church callings that placed me in the role of counselor, confidant, and judge, I have witnessed firsthand the unhappiness fomented by people who have been unwilling to forgive those who have deliberately or unwittingly "trespassed" against them. Some of these grudges have lasted for decades, literally altering the personality and life's experience of the unforgiving.

I am reminded of the classic story by French writer Guy de Maupassant. He related the life-altering experience of a simple peasant named Hauchecome who turned a defining moment into a personal nightmare for himself and perhaps for others as well.

While walking through the public square of his village one day, Hauchecome saw a piece of string lying on the cobblestones. Without much forethought he leaned over and picked up the string, placing it in his pocket.

Unknown to him, the village harness maker, with whom he had previously had a disagreement, had observed this seemingly unimportant action.

Later that same day a purse was reported missing, and the harness maker accused Hauchecome of picking it up and pocketing it. He was arrested and brought before the mayor, where he protested his innocence, showing his accusers the piece of string he had placed in his pocket. However, his protests provoked mocking laughter rather than exoneration. Surely he did not expect his accusers to believe this fabled excuse of "a piece of string." They demanded the return of the lost purse.

The following day the purse was found, and Hauchecome was absolved of any wrongdoing. However, he refused to accept the apology and allowed the incident to embitter and canker his soul. In a spirit that became increasingly resentful of the humiliation he had suffered, he thought and spoke of little else. "A piece of string! A piece of string!" he would say as he repeated over and over his story to any unlucky enough to be stopped by him.

His obsession with the injustice done to him led to a neglect of his farm and ultimately to ill health and death. Unforgiving to the last, his final words in mortality were, "A piece of string! A piece of string!" (*The Works of Guy de Maupassant* [Roslyn, N.Y.: Black's Reader Service, 1972], 34–38).

"Do not let yesterday hold tomorrow hostage!" cautioned Elder Neal A. Maxwell (*Ensign*, May 1982, 39).

The parents of Jeralee Underwood understood this inspired counsel. Their daughter was a bright, happy young pre-teen living in Pocatello, Idaho. One fateful day the eleven-year-old left her house to collect payments for the newspaper she delivered. She never returned home.

For days thousands of volunteers searched and scoured the surrounding area in an effort to find the missing girl. The uncertainty of her whereabouts finally came to a sad conclusion when it was discovered that she had been abducted and brutally murdered by an evil man. The recovery of her body horrified the community. Some were so angry they spoke of vigilante vengeance. Yet Jeff and Joyce Underwood, the grieving parents, were calmed by the Spirit of God.

Facing the news media, the Underwoods expressed their gratitude to the thousands of volunteers who had helped in the search effort and to the many who had extended love, prayers, and support through this most difficult time. They expressed their gratitude to God for helping them find their daughter's remains. "I know our Heavenly Father has heard and answered our prayers," said the mother. "[God] has brought our daughter back to us." The father added, "We no longer have doubt about where she is."

In a moment that mattered very much, Joyce Underwood then gave quite a lesson in forgiveness and faith. "I have learned a lot about love this week, and I also know there is a lot of hate. I have looked at the love and want to feel that love, and not the hate. We can forgive" (in James E. Faust, *Finding Light in a Dark World* [Salt Lake City: Deseret Book, 1995], 47–48).

In the wake of a terrible tragedy these wonderful

parents, who by worldly standards appeared to have every justification for bitterness, chose the higher road. They chose peace of mind over despair, hate, and anger.

So, too, have others who have faced similar anguishing moments that tried their faith. One of the most heinous acts of cruelty committed against civilized people was the terrorist attack of September 11, 2001. Almost 3,000 innocent victims lost their lives on that day, and thousands more were injured. Emotionally scarred children were left without parents, wives and husbands were deprived of their spouses, and families lost brothers and sisters as a result of the hatred of a handful of evil and conspiring men.

Yet out of the carnage came charity. Stranger turned to stranger in an outreach of love and helpfulness. And the estranged, those whose resentment of another had caused them to build and remain behind walls of rejection and isolation, softened their hearts and extended the olive leaf of reconciliation towards those from whom they had taken offense.

Yes, there is a sacred obligation to ferret out and bring to justice the perpetrators of these evil acts and to prevent them from further terrorizing the innocent. But it is important not to become consumed with anger and hatred. On the first anniversary of her husband Jason's death, Sandy Dahl, the widow of the pilot of United Airlines Flight 93—the hijacked plane that crashed in a field in Pennsylvania—said, "Life is short, and there is no time for hate."

Similar sentiments were expressed by the surviving

spouses of other victims of the abominations of 9/11. Additionally, President George W. Bush told a grieving nation, "Grief and tragedy and hatred are only for a time. Goodness, remembrance and love have no end."

Even young children understand the peace that can come as one turns away from bitterness, resentment, and soul-consuming anger. An example is found in the attitude of the eight-year-old son of slain law-enforcement officer Fred House. In an act of hatred against The Church of Jesus Christ of Latter-day Saints, a man had set fire to a church building and then, with his associates, barricaded himself in a thirteen-day standoff with the law. In the course of trying to capture the man, Officer House was shot and killed. Following the funeral his young boy said to his mother, "Mommy, I'll never hate those people who shot Daddy. I don't want to live on the dark side of life—like they showed in the movie 'Star Wars'" (*Deseret News*, Jan. 28, 1989, B1).

On several occasions President Boyd K. Packer has related the story of the man whose wife died as a result of an infection she contracted from the doctor who treated her while delivering her first child. It seems the mother was suffering severe complications on the night of the baby's birth, and the situation was so desperate that upon arriving at the home the doctor had acted in haste to save the lives of both the mother and the baby. He had not taken the time to properly sanitize his hands, which carried the germs from patients he had treated earlier that evening.

The man, whose name was John, despaired over his

wife's death and blamed the doctor, demanding that he not be allowed to practice medicine anymore. His focus turned from grieving over his wife's loss to resentment of the doctor. His bitterness became all consuming. One night he was invited to visit with the stake president—his spiritual shepherd. "John, leave it alone," said this spiritual adviser. "Nothing you do about it will bring her back. Anything you do will make it worse. John, leave it alone."

As hard as it was, John was obedient to his leader and prayed for a change of heart.

Years later, as he recounted this experience, John said, "I was an old man before I finally understood. It was not until I was an old man that I could finally see a poor country doctor—overworked, underpaid, run ragged from patient to patient, with little proper medicine, no hospital, few instruments. He struggled to save lives, and succeeded for the most part.

"He had come in a moment of crisis when two lives hung in the balance and had acted without delay.

"I was an old man," he repeated, "before finally I understood. I would have ruined my life . . . and the lives of others" (*Ensign*, Nov. 1977, 60; Nov. 1987, 17–18).

What an astute insight! "I would have ruined my life *and* the lives of others." Anger, hatred, and revenge do not exist in a vacuum. There is always more than one victim when forgiveness is withheld.

Choosing between being forgiving and being unforgiving can have eternal consequences. The Lord declared, "I say unto you, that ye ought to forgive one another; for he that forgiveth not his brother his trespasses standeth condemned before the Lord; for there remaineth in him the greater sin" (D&C 64:9). In commenting on this scriptural admonition, Elder Theodore M. Burton said, "I take that to mean that it is a greater sin to refuse to forgive a person than it is to commit the sin" (*Ensign*, May 1983, 72).

We may not control what another says or does, but we do control our reaction and, therefore, our destiny. Consider the case of a Hawaiian father who, together with his family, embraced the restored gospel of Jesus Christ and joined The Church of Jesus Christ of Latter-day Saints in the early 1900s. He faithfully attended church meetings and looked forward to the day when he and his family could enter the holy temple and there be sealed as an eternal unit under the priesthood authority restored by the ancient prophet Elijah (see D&C 110:13–16).

Then came a moment that mattered so much. A test! One of his daughters was stricken with an unknown disease and was taken to a hospital for treatment. The family went to church the following Sunday in a spirit of prayer in behalf of the young girl and anticipating the support of their fellow branch members.

The father and one of his sons took their place at the sacrament table to assist in blessing and passing the sacred emblems. After breaking the bread, the father knelt and began to utter the prayer of blessing on the bread. Suddenly, the branch president interrupted the man and shouted, "Stop! You can't touch the sacrament. Your daughter has an unknown disease. Leave immediately while someone else fixes new sacrament bread. We can't have you here. Go!"

Shocked, disappointed, and dismayed, the stunned father arose from his knees, and sensing the anxiety of the congregation, gathered his family and silently left the chapel. Without a word the family made its way home, where they all sat in a circle on the floor. "We will be silent until I am ready to speak," said the visibly shaken and angry father.

"What would he do? What would he say?" The children and his wife wondered. His decision on this momentous occasion had eternal consequences not only for his family but also for generations unborn—his future posterity. Would the actions of the branch president be allowed to determine this family's destiny? Would faith be discarded and resentment and revenge take center stage in their lives?

The father sat silently with eyes closed, perhaps at first in personal contemplation but then in searching prayer. What should he do? His heart began to soften, and the tears began to flow. The Spirit had touched him, and the healing process had begun. Finally subdued, the father opened his eyes and said, "I am now ready to speak. Listen carefully." Turning to his wife he said, "I love you!" Then he made the same declaration to each child. "I love all of you, and I want us to be together forever as a family. And the only way that can be is for all of us to be good members of The Church of Jesus Christ of Latter-day Saints and be sealed by His holy priesthood in the temple. This is not the branch president's church. It is the Church of Jesus

Christ. We will not let any man or any amount of hurt or embarrassment or pride keep us from being together forever. Next Sunday we will go back to church. We will stay by ourselves until our daughter's sickness is known, but we will go back."

What an eternal perspective!

In time the daughter was cured, and the family went to the temple to receive the anticipated blessings. And the children remained faithful and were sealed in the temple to their own spouses, and their children were born in the covenant their parents had entered into at a sacred altar in a holy place. How tragic would have been the consequences had the father and now grandfather been unforgiving in a moment that mattered so much for him and his family.

To be unforgiving not only fosters unhappiness but also forges shackles that prevent progression.

Chapter 8

TRUE AT ALL TIMES

❖ ❖ ❖ ❖ ❖ ❖ ❖ ❖ ❖ ❖

"They were all young men, and they were exceedingly valiant for courage, . . . but behold, this was not all—they were men who were true at all times in whatsoever thing they were entrusted" (Alma 53:20).

This description of the two thousand young Lamanite men known as Helaman's stripling warriors stands as a model for all to follow. In defining moments, when choices must be made between courageously keeping our standards or buckling to the pressures of the moment, the clarion call is "Be true at all times!"

One young man who remained true to his standards in the face of peer pressure was a young Latter-day Saint named Bob Brown. The seventeen-year-old youth approached the family pharmacist, Mr. Jones, and asked if he could do some part-time work for him in order to help pay for the medicine Bob's family needed but found difficult to pay for.

Although he really didn't need the help, the pharmacist was impressed with the young man's willingness to help his family and agreed to let him work part-time. At the end of the first day, Mr. Jones handed Bob an envelope containing the agreed-upon wages—twelve dollars. Bob put $1.20 in his pocket and returned the other $10.80 to his new employer, asking the man to put that money toward the family's bill.

"At that moment some of Bob's friends came by and asked him to attend a movie with them. He said he couldn't, that he had to go home. They continued to tease him to go with them until finally he informed them firmly that he didn't have any money and couldn't go with them. Mr. Jones, observing all of this, was about to intervene . . . to offer money to Bob, when one of the boys who had playfully jostled him heard the twenty cents rattle in Bob's pocket. The bantering began again, because obviously he did have some money. Quietly Bob finally said, 'Look, guys, I do have a little money but it isn't mine; it's my tithing. Now take off, will you please. I need to get home to see how Mom's doing.'"

Bob Brown was true to his trust. As a result of observing Bob's courageous stand in the face of his friends' pressures, Mr. Jones decided to investigate the religion that would produce such an outstanding young man. The man and members of his family soon received testimonies of the truth and joined The Church of Jesus Christ of Latter-day Saints, all because one young man was *true at all times* (see Conference Report, Oct. 1977, 55–56).

Bishop Victor L. Brown told of a young Latter-day Saint who was the only member of the Church on board an atomic submarine based in Scotland. "As this young Church member was assigned to his station on his first cruise, he found that other crewmen had plastered the walls in his area with suggestive pictures of scantily clad women. This offended him. He took all the pictures down and destroyed them. He was conscious of the probable reaction of the other men but, nevertheless, had the courage to do what he thought he should. Not one picture was put up again. . . . He learned an important lesson—generally speaking, others will show respect for one who has the courage of his or her convictions and isn't afraid to do what he feels is right" ("A Light on a Hill," *New Era*, Sept. 1980, 4).

Often some will test another to see if he will bend to pressure. When one tactic doesn't work, these advocates of evil will frequently try different approaches on the satanic theory that "everyone has his price." This is the strategy Satan used in seeking to tempt the Savior following the Master's forty-day fast (see Matthew 4:1–11).

Each time Jesus withstood the tempter's offer, the devil countered with a new proposal, hoping to find a price this sinless Son of God would accept. Fortunately for us, Jesus was the master of the moment. We shall be redeemed from the grave and, through our faithfulness, from the clutches of hell because Christ was true at all times to His divine nature and mission.

Few will face the devil directly as we square off in the fight with temptation. However, we will constantly confront those who use the tempter's tactics and act in his behalf. Consider the experience of one faithful Latter-day Saint teenager:

"She was the only member of the Church in her class in school. She was a popular young lady with the boys and had many opportunities to go out on dates. The boys in her class did not live by the standards she had been taught in our Church. She made the decision to tell every boy who asked her for a date what standards she lived by. If she were to date them, they would be expected to conduct themselves in accordance with her standards. She would get such a commitment from them before she accepted a date. One day the big campus football hero came up to her before the most special dance of the year and said, 'You know, I would ask you to go to the dance with me if you would lower your standards just a little.'

"There was no hesitation in her voice as she replied, 'If I would go out with you, I would be lowering my standards'" (L. Tom Perry, "Making the Right Decisions," *Ensign*, Nov. 1979, 36).

This young lady was true at all times because she had made the decision to do right *in advance* of the moment of temptation.

A small boy living on farmland in Arizona years ago learned the importance of advance decisions. He said to himself, "I, Spencer Kimball, will never taste any form of liquor. I, Spencer Kimball, will never touch tobacco. I will never drink coffee, nor will I ever touch tea—not because I can explain why I shouldn't, except that the Lord said not to. . . .

"I made up my mind then, as a little boy; 'I will never touch those things.' And so, *having made up my mind, it was easy to follow it*, and I did not yield [to future temptations]."

Years later, this same boy, grown to be a prophet of God, said, "If every boy and girl . . . would make up his or her mind, 'I will not yield,' then no matter what the temptation is: 'I made up my mind. That's settled'" (*Church News*, Oct. 4, 1975, 16).

An irrevocable decision to do what is right, to be true at all times, affects not only our own lives but also the lives of others.

Joe was stationed in Tehran, the capital of Iran, as a member of a military mission some years ago. He was a Latter-day Saint who had been given the serviceman's edition of the Book of Mormon and a book called *Principles of the Gospel* before leaving the United States.

Joe was anxious to learn the Farsi language and thought a good way of doing this would be to work with children. He found a boy and a girl who agreed to help him learn their native language if he would teach them English. Joe didn't have any basic texts in English, so he used his LDS books to teach the children English. In the process, he taught them about the Word of Wisdom and other beliefs and practices of the Church.

One day he was invited by the children to visit the home of their well-to-do uncle. Joe was treated very hospitably, and he and the children had a wonderful visit with the man. Finally, the uncle excused himself and returned with a silver tray that contained a silver decanter of wine and two tiny silver cups. He placed the tray on a beautiful bronze table and proceeded to pour some wine into the two thimble-sized cups.

The serviceman was in a dilemma. As a Latter-day Saint he knew he should not drink the wine. But he also knew that partaking of the liquid was a custom of courtesy in the country in which he was a guest. "What shall I do?" he thought to himself. "I don't want to offend my host."

Thinking the thimbleful of wine such a small thing,

Regarding those who must patiently wait for the blessing of marriage and eternal companionship, an apostle of the Lord Jesus Christ has said: "Don't abandon hope for a temple marriage.

"If you are single and haven't identified a solid prospect for celestial marriage, live for it. Pray for it. Expect it in the timetable of the Lord. *Do not compromise your standards in any way that would rule out that blessing on this or the other side of the veil.* The Lord knows the intent of your heart. His prophets have stated that you will have that blessing as you consistently live to qualify for it" (Elder Richard G. Scott in *Ensign*, May 1999, 27; emphasis added).

In all things, one makes matters worse by compromising standards, giving in to pressure to do the wrong thing, or turning from faith and hope to despondency, discouragement, and despair. When adversity and disappointment come, don't let your knees buckle in despair; let them bend in prayer. Affirm your faith in God's love, knowing that what is best for your eternal growth and salvation is what He desires for you.

In moments of challenge, we would do well to follow the example of the much-tried but patient and faithful Job, who following great adversity "fell down upon the ground, and worshipped, and said, . . . blessed be the name of the Lord. In all this Job sinned not, nor charged God foolishly" (Job 1:20–22).

the serviceman bowed at the altar of social pressure and joined the uncle in a toast to each other's health. It is a sad irony that the same toast that was supposed to bring good physical health was responsible for an onset of spiritual sickness.

Detecting an almost immediate change in the atmosphere of the home, the Latter-day Saint excused himself and left with the children. The little girl started to cry and said, "Joe, why did you do it? Why did you do it? Why did you take that drink?"

Seeking to justify his action, Joe replied that it was only a thimbleful. Its alcoholic effects were so minimal that they certainly couldn't have harmed him

"Well," the young boy replied, "that doesn't make any difference. Uncle said you would do it. We told him about the Word of Wisdom and he said, 'Those Americans talk about a lot of things but they don't believe them!' We told him that you really did, but you didn't."

The children's words and their disappointment in him seared his soul with anguish. He would have given anything to be able to repeat that momentous moment. But it was too late. He could not reclaim what he had lost—the respect of the children—for he had failed to be true at all times (see Theodore M. Burton, "Tickling the Tiger," *BYU Speeches of the Year*, Jan. 17, 1961, 7–9).

In a momentous moment the now sorrowful serviceman would have done well to reflect on the words of the Lord to another who had tasted the bitter fruits of having given in to the pressures of mortal man as opposed to God's counsel: "Behold, you should not have feared man more than God. . . . You should have been faithful" (D&C 3:7–8).

Sorrow follows the setting aside of standards just as surely as night follows the day. On the other hand, there is great joy and satisfaction in being true at all times.

Consider the case of thirteen-year-old Andrew Flosdorf. He was among the select few who were participating in a national spelling bee, vying for fame and prizes. Andrew had been asked to spell the word "ukulele" and had responded to the approval of the judges. However, young Andrew discovered he had actually misspelled the word. The judges had incorrectly heard his pronunciation of a letter. He called the mistake to their attention and was eliminated from the competition. Asked why he had informed the judges of the error, the boy said: "I didn't want to feel like a slime. After all, the first rule of Scouting is honesty" (used by permission of United Press International).

Andrew did not leave the contest with a tangible trophy for spelling excellence, but he did return home with the joy of a clear conscience, for he had been true.

Another boy who was true was Bobby Palacio, a fourteen-year-old ninth-grader. Bobby had trained and dreamed of breaking the school record of 2.1 seconds for the rope climb. Although the boy had tied the record, his heart was set on improving his climb. On the second of three allowed attempts, Bobby practically flew up the rope, and the stopwatch showed 2.0 seconds, a new school record.

After the boy had descended the rope to the cheers of

the crowd in the gymnasium, the coach asked the all-important question: "Bobby, did you touch the board at the fifteen-foot mark?" Only Bobby had the answer. If he had missed, it would have been so easy to have lied. None but Bobby would know. The lad was true. He sadly shook his head. "No!" He had missed the mark.

The coach, with eyes as misty as Bobby's, turned to the crestfallen crowd of well-wishers and said, "This boy has not set a record in the rope climb. No, he has set a much finer record for you and everyone to strive for. He has told the simple truth." Turning to the disappointed boy the coach said, "I'm proud of you. You have just set a record many athletes never attain."

Happily for Bobby, there was one more chance at the record. This time he not only touched the board at the fifteen-foot mark, but he did it in 1.9 seconds, a new record (from *California Teacher's Journal*, as quoted by Victor L. Brown, "Make Yourself an Honest Man," *Speeches of the Year* [1973] [Provo: BYU Press, 1974], 155–56).

Not all have another chance like Bobby. The young spelling-bee enthusiast didn't. Nevertheless, neither the promised reward nor recognition should determine whether or not one is true to the trust placed in him or her by others or oneself.

"The getting of treasures [rewards or recognition] by a lying tongue is a vanity [something that is empty or useless]" (Proverbs 21:6). Of what value would a record or trophy have been to either Bobby or Andrew if it had been obtained through lying? It would have served as a minor monument to deceit, a constant reminder that his conscience was not clear. Fortunately, both boys were true in soul-stretching, defining moments.

Being true, having integrity, is a way of life. It is a habit.

Elder S. Dilworth Young, who served many years as a General Authority, had been a professional Scout before his call to full-time service in The Church of Jesus Christ of Latter-day Saints. He had both learned and taught the principle of being honest and true.

One night he was driving home late, anxious to take care of his sick wife. As the concerned husband pressed the car's accelerator to the floor, the vehicle reached a speed of more than seventy miles per hour. It was at this point that he noticed the flashing red lights of the patrol car behind him. He pulled over to the side and waited for the inevitable ticket and lecture.

As the officer approached, Elder Young said, "I guess you're arresting me for speeding."

The officer replied, "Yes, you were doing better than sixty miles an hour."

Speaking with uncharacteristic honesty for one who had just been pulled over for speeding, Elder Young said, "I was doing better than *seventy* miles an hour." He then explained that he was in a hurry to get home to his sick wife and would be glad to pay the fine but pleaded with the officer to give him the ticket *quickly* so he could get home to his ailing wife.

The officer surprised Elder Young by stating he was not going to give him anything but a warning ticket. He then admonished him to stay within the speed limit and drive carefully the rest of the way home. The officer stuck out his hand and said, "My name's Bybee. I used to be one of your Scouts."

As Elder Young drove home he thought to himself, "What if I'd lied to him? He knew I was doing seventy . . . and he knew I was his Scout executive years before. . . . If I had not told him the exact truth or tried to hedge at all he would have lost respect. . . . I would have had no influence on that man ever again" ("Living Flames, Not Dead Ashes," *1977 Devotional Speeches of the Year* [Provo: BYU Press, 1978], 99; emphasis added).

Because S. Dilworth Young was true at all times, he maintained the respect of a former Scout and brought greater meaning to the Scout's promise to be honest at all times. He showed that honesty and integrity are not something people just talk about or live at convenient points of life. Being honest is a habit, a natural response of one who is true at all times.

There will be moments, such as that experienced by the speeding driver, when it would be so easy to stray slightly from being true. Our response in such situations is voluntary. It comes without direct pressure being applied by another person. For example, the officer did not *ask* Elder Young how fast he was going. That information was voluntarily given.

There are other times when intense pressure is applied to get us to deviate from strict standards. A young nurse in an operating room experienced this kind of pressure. It was her first full day of assisting surgeons in the room that served as the stage for life-and-death dramas. At the conclusion of one operation she said to the doctor, "You've removed eleven sponges, but we used twelve."

The surgeon quickly said, "I've removed them all. We'll close the incision now!"

"No," the nurse persisted. "There is one sponge still in the patient's body."

The doctor said, "I will take the responsibility. We will now suture the incision."

In a defining moment, the nurse held to her standards. She was true to the trust placed in her. Resisting the pressure from the doctor, she held her ground and demanded that he carefully search the cavity cut in the body to find the missing sponge.

At this moment the face of the physician brightened. He smiled and said, "You will do." He then lifted his foot showing the nurse the missing sponge. "He had been testing her for her integrity—and she had it" (excerpted with permission from "A Foolproof Formula for Success" by Arthur Gordon; copyright © 1974 by Arthur Gordon).

The nurse could not be swayed from the standards of right. When the crisis came and a critical choice had to be made, she held her ground. Wrong choices are often the result of inadequate preparation, of not having practiced a true principle.

The Book of Mormon relates the experience of the subjects of the wicked King Noah. He lived a lecherous life, and many of his people followed his evil example. One day the king discovered that his kingdom was about to be attacked by an army of Lamanites. The monarch warned his people to flee the invading army. As they fled, they discovered that their escape was slowed because of the number of women and children in the group. Seeing the distance narrow between him and his enemies, the king ordered the men to leave their wives and children and save their own lives.

Many refused to leave their loved ones and remained behind. Others, however, chose to follow the king, selfishly seeking their own safety while forsaking those who had loved and trusted them (see Mosiah 19:1–2). This was not a one-time point-of-panic decision on the part of Noah and his people. Each acted on the basis of previously established patterns of behavior.

Elder Delbert L. Stapley, a former member of the Quorum of the Twelve Apostles, made an observation that applies to the experience of Noah and his followers and is worth pondering as we consider our own course of life: "It is not in the moments of great test and trial that character is built. That is only when it is displayed" (Conference Report, Oct. 1974, 25).

One young farm boy displayed his true character in a different kind of setting. He was not beset by those trying to get him to lower his standards of conduct. His challenge was a request made by his father in a defining moment.

The boy had just returned from a long day of working in the hay fields. He was tired, dirty, and hungry and both needed and deserved a rest and some food. His father met him with a request that he go to town on an errand. The impulse of his physical body was to refuse the request, but this boy's character prevailed. His spirit responded positively to the request for help. He knew if he did not walk the two miles to town and complete the errand himself that his ailing father would have to go.

The father said, "Thank you, my son; you've always been a good boy to me."

Upon returning from the errand, the boy was surprised to find all the farmhands gathered at the door of the house instead of doing their chores. With tears rolling down his cheeks, one of the men informed the faithful son that his father had suffered a heart attack and was dead. His last spoken words were of the boy, who was true at all times (see John H. Vandenberg, "The Presiding Bishop Talks to Youth About Respect," *Improvement Era*, Feb. 1968, 49).

Those who have character are true at all times.

Chapter 9

ON MY HONOR

◆　◆　◆　◆　◆　◆　◆　◆　◆

"On my honor I will do my best . . ." These familiar
words from the Scout oath have been repeated by millions
of boys since Lord Baden-Powell instituted this personal
pledge of integrity nearly a century ago. Yet his was not the
first effort at formalizing a pledge of honor. From the time
of Adam and Eve mortals have bound themselves to
covenant conduct. In truth, agreeing to abide by sacred
covenants with Deity predates mortality.

In this life oaths are administered to those elected or
appointed to offices of public trust. In business and legal
affairs people attest to the truth by affixing their signatures
on documents. The signers of the Declaration of
Independence pledged their honor to that historic docu-
ment. And as citizens of the nation born from that decisive decision, Americans pledge their allegiance to their
flag and government.

Husbands and wives promise their love, loyalty, and
fidelity to one another in ceremonies involving sacred
covenants. And even small children seek the trust and
confidence of one another with the words "I promise."

Holders of the holy Melchizedek Priesthood have
received that authority with an oath and a covenant to
honor and respect that sacred trust (see D&C 84:33–42).
President Gordon B. Hinckley once suggested that boys

and men who hold either the Aaronic or Melchizedek Priesthood might well repeat the following pledge: "On my honor I will do my best to magnify the priesthood of God which has been conferred upon me" (*Ensign*, May 1989, 46).

Anciently, Nephi pledged his honor to perform his duty by declaring, "As the Lord liveth [swearing on the very life of Deity], and as we live [pledging his own life and that of his brothers], we will not go . . . until we have accomplished the thing which the Lord hath commanded us" (1 Nephi 3:15).

Honor implies trust. Recall how Nephi and his brothers totally trusted Zoram once he had given his word of honor to them (see 1 Nephi 4:37). "My word is my bond" is another phrase that emphasizes personal honor. Honor is central to character. Elder Marvin J. Ashton observed, "A pledge of 'on my honor I will do my best,' either in writing or when self-enforced, can make the difference in character development" (*Ensign*, May 1987, 66).

President James E. Faust shared an experience from his early life wherein his mother helped teach her young son the importance of honor. The children in the Faust home shared in performing household chores, and one evening young Jim had agreed to wash the dishes and clean the kitchen while his mother attended to a sick neighbor. The boy got distracted with other things, and when his mother returned home she found the chores undone. She looked at her son with a disappointed look and said just three words: "On my honor." President Faust said that phrase stung him more than any punishment he might have received. "That day," he said, "I resolved that I would never give my mother cause to repeat those words to me again" (*Ensign*, May 1998, 44).

In a sense, the boy Jim Faust developed an honor code in his early life that led him on the road to the impeccable character for which he is now known as President James E. Faust, a counselor in the First Presidency of The Church of Jesus Christ of Latter-day Saints.

Brigham Young University is known for its Honor Code. Prior to being accepted, each prospective student signs a pledge whereby he or she agrees to abide by high standards of conduct. The Honor Code had its beginning with the school's first president, Karl G. Maeser. He was called by President Brigham Young to establish a Church academy in Provo, Utah, and was given the charge that he "should teach not even the multiplication tables or the alphabet without the aid and inspiration of our Heavenly Father."

Acting on faith, this German immigrant commenced his task and soon had his first twenty-nine students enrolled. At the first meeting, Karl G. Maeser gave the following profound but concise charge to the students regarding the code of conduct: "We trust you all; we give you our confidence; we hope you will do nothing to weaken that confidence. *We put you on your word of honor*" (in Conference Report, Oct. 1958, 124; emphasis added).

How wonderful the world would be if all could be trusted to live by such a code!

Cheating, lying, breaking pledges, going back on one's

word, dishonesty in any form—all of these unworthy actions diminish one's personal character and reduce civilization to a lower level of living. Character flaws not only hurt the weak individual who has developed them by succumbing to sin and the low road but also hurt family members, friends, and even strangers who are affected by such flaws.

Consider, for example, one who foolishly cheats in order to receive a professional license. By so doing he or she places others in jeopardy by potentially subjecting them to services that are not only less than they should and could be but are potentially dangerous. Most have heard the oft-cited question posed regarding an ill-qualified surgeon: "Would you want to be operated on by a doctor who had cheated his or her way through medical school?"

Years ago, a group of beginning medical students was taking an examination. The honor system was in place, and there were no monitors pacing the aisles to ensure that cheating did not occur. However, soon after the professor left the room, some dishonorable students began to pull out cheat-sheets from their pockets. Suddenly, in a defining moment, a tall, lanky student stood in the back of the room and spoke: "I left my hometown and put my wife and three little babies in an upstairs apartment and worked very hard to get into medical school. And I'll turn in the first one of you who cheats, and *you better believe it!*" (*Ensign*, Nov. 1996, 42).

Sometimes honor requires courageous action on the part of *one* to stop dishonorable actions on the part of others.

A young shepherd boy was tending his flock of sheep one day when he was approached by a stranger with a proposition. The man asked the boy for directions to the nearest village, but he wanted the boy to lead him there. The lad replied that he could not leave the sheep, for some might wander and get lost in his absence. "Well, what of that!" replied the man. "They are not *your* sheep, and the loss of one or two would not matter to your master. I will give you more money than you have earned in a year if you will lead me to the village."

The shepherd boy, true to his trust, steadfastly declined, in spite of ever-increasing pressure from the stranger.

Finally, the man said, "I see you are a good faithful boy. I will not forget you. Give me directions and I will try to make it on my own."

The man turned out to be a grand duke who was so impressed with the boy's integrity that he later provided for the lad's education and professional development (see "A Faithful Shepherd Boy," in *Moral Stories for Little Folks* [Salt Lake City: Juvenile Instructor Office (1891)], 11–13).

While not all acts of moral courage, of being true to one's word of honor, will be rewarded like the young shepherd boy, all such actions will have a significant impact on one's character and the ultimate reward to be received at the hands of God.

I have a feeling that honor might be displayed most often under anonymous circumstances when no mortal eyes are really conscious of our conduct and only we ourselves know if we are keeping our promises or acting in a true and honorable way.

Consider the circumstances of a twelve-year-old boy in the Philippines named Julius. He had gone to school without eating breakfast one morning. During recess he decided to run to the nearby store and get something to eat. He ran to the store and quickly consumed the food before running back to his class.

As he sat listening to his teacher, he suddenly realized he had not paid for the food. He had been in such a hurry that this had been forgotten. Without hesitation, Julius jumped up and ran from the classroom. He apologized to the store owner, paid for his snack, and returned to the classroom. The teacher demanded to know why he had left without seeking permission. When the boy explained what had happened, the teacher put her arm around this honorable student and said to the class, "I want you to be honest like Julius" (*Ensign*, Nov. 1991, 13).

It is possible that not even the storekeeper knew of the unpaid debt. Certainly, no one in Julius' class knew. But the boy did! And he kept his honor!

Honor is lost when one succumbs to the siren song of such phrases as "No one will know" or "It's not going to hurt anybody!" Heavenly Father and the Savior will *always* know. And so will *you!*

On *my* honor I will do my best, keep my covenants, and not break promises.

Some years ago a troubled young father went to visit with President N. Eldon Tanner of the First Presidency for some counsel. The young man explained that he was in financial difficulty. It seems that if he met his obligation on a pledge he had made, he would be unable to make his house payment and stood in danger of losing the house. "What shall I do?" he asked.

President Tanner, who was known in business circles as "Mr. Integrity," didn't hesitate in responding. "Keep your agreement," he replied.

"Even if it costs me my home?" the man asked.

President Tanner replied, "I am not talking about your home. I am talking about your agreement [could we say 'your honor']; and I think your wife would rather have a husband who would keep his word, meet his obligations, keep his pledges or his covenants, and have to rent a home, than to have a home with a husband who will not keep his covenants and his pledges" (Conference Report, Oct. 1966, 99).

The Savior asked, "What is a man profited, if he shall gain the whole world, and lose his own soul? or what shall a man give in exchange for his soul?" (Matthew 16:26).

Being honorable in keeping our pledges to God is critical to any seeking to develop a celestial character. Promises of obedience and trust were made to our Father in Heaven prior to coming to this earth as mortal beings. Those promises are reaffirmed and perhaps expanded in this life as we enter into covenants with Deity through the waters of baptism, partaking of the sacrament, ordination to the priesthood, and receiving the sacred ordinances of the temple.

Among the covenant commitments made by members of The Church of Jesus Christ of Latter-day Saints is the payment of honest tithes and offerings. "Paying tithing is not a token gift we are somehow charitably bestowing upon God," said Elder Jeffrey R. Holland. "Paying tithing is discharging a debt" (*Ensign*, Nov. 2001, 34). Yet the Church is not a collection agency. Contributions are voluntary and must come from upright hearts.

Someone once said that tithing is not paid with money but with faith.

Jack was the father of a family struggling with economic challenges that tested their faith. He called a family council and told his wife and children that if they paid their tithing that month they would run out of money for food by the 20th. The father felt that food should come first and wanted to skip paying their tithing that month. However, the faith of the children was such that they insisted that the Lord be paid first.

As a result of their faithfulness in keeping their covenants, this little family experienced what might be considered a modern-day parallel to a well-known Old Testament story. Remember the incident when the prophet Elijah asked a widow of Zarephath to feed him before looking after the needs of herself and her son? The little bit of flour and oil the woman had was just enough to bake a small cake for the two of them. How could she make this sacrifice! Yet an inspired prophet of God promised her that "the barrel of meal shall not waste, neither shall the cruse of oil fail" (1 Kings 17:14). The obedient woman reaped the rewards of her sacrifice, for the prophet's promise was fulfilled.

In the case of the modern-day family faced with the

prospects of going without food, the Lord similarly provided. Several days after paying their tithing, a knock came on the door of Jack's home. To the delight of the children and the relief of Jack and his wife, there stood a young couple with a gift of food. Truly, their own barrel had not wasted nor their cruse failed (*Ensign*, Nov. 1996, 44–45). They were blessed because they honored their pledge to the Lord.

While the God of Heaven has not always promised relief from suffering, He has promised that He will always be there to strengthen us and support us through whatever trials may come. His promises are sure! His word is true!

Perhaps this might be illustrated with an earthy example. In 1989 a terrible earthquake in Armenia killed more than thirty thousand people in less than five minutes. A frantic father went to the location of his young son's school only to find the building reduced to a pile of rubble. He reflected on a promise he had made the boy: "No matter what, I'll always be there for you!"

Anxiously, he began to dig in the area where he knew his son's classroom to have been. Brick by brick he removed the rubble in his search for his son. After thirty-eight hours of digging, the father heard the faint cry of his son's voice. "Armand," he cried out, "is that you?" "Dad! It's me, Dad!" came the faint reply. As the father continued digging he heard his boy say, "I told the other kids not to worry. I told 'em that if you were alive, you'd save me and when you saved me, they'd be saved" (*Ensign*, May 2001, 46).

The faith of a boy in his father's word.

Trust!

How much more should we trust in and rely upon the words of our Eternal Father and in the words and promises of His Beloved Son, our Savior, Jesus Christ! One of the attributes of Deity is the absolute trust we can place in anything God says. If we are to be saved, then we must trust in His word. If we are to follow the Savior's admonition to be like Him and His holy Father (see 3 Nephi 12:48; 27:27), then we too must be honorable and always be true to our word, keeping our covenants.

Chapter 10

OBEDIENCE: CLOSE TO
BEING A CURE-ALL

❖ ❖ ❖ ❖ ❖ ❖ ❖ ❖ ❖ ❖

On a stormy night some years ago in Tasmania, a huge barge accidentally slammed into piers holding a bridge in place. The force of the collision caused a span of the bridge to collapse, knocking out the lights on the structure. Certain death awaited the unwary drivers who proceeded in the darkness along the bridge toward the chasm that led to the turbulent waters below.

A car carrying the Ling family was proceeding toward the precipice when it was passed by a speeding vehicle that suddenly disappeared into a black void. Mr. Ling slammed on his brakes and skidded to a stop just inches from the drop-off. The man quickly got his family out of the car and took them to a safer place on the side of the bridge. He then ran down the road frantically waving his arms at oncoming cars to warn them of the danger ahead. On that fateful night many lives were saved because of the drivers who heeded the warnings of this "watchman on the tower." Unfortunately, some lives were also lost because drivers disregarded the warnings, swerving around the waving man and proceeding to their deaths.

This story reminds me of the dream Father Lehi had of the tree of life (see 1 Nephi 8). This ancient seer was shown a strait and narrow path that led to the safety of this spiritually symbolic tree. Lehi also saw mists of darkness that arose to shroud the path, causing some to wander into forbidden paths that led to their destruction. He saw a rod of iron that, if held, kept people on the safe path. After joyously partaking of the fruit of the tree himself, Lehi stood as a sentinel and beckoned to his family to join him in the safety of the tree. Some of his family obediently followed their father's admonition, joining him in joyously partaking of the fruit of the tree. But, sadly, others rejected the invitation, placing their spiritual lives in jeopardy as they wandered into forbidden and dangerous paths.

The issue of obedience versus disobedience is at the heart of our spiritual well-being. Elder Boyd K. Packer observed, "Obedience is a powerful spiritual medicine. It comes close to being a cure-all" (*Ensign*, Nov. 1977, 60).

I believe that the prophet Alma stated this same principle, but in a negative way, when he declared, "Wickedness [disobedience] never was happiness" (Alma 41:10). Samuel the Lamanite prophet also taught this truth when he declared to the wicked Nephites that they had "sought for happiness in doing iniquity, which thing is contrary to the nature of that righteousness which is in our great and Eternal Head" (Helaman 13:38).

Inner peace and true happiness come from obedience. Those who "break the rules" or see how close they can come to a line without stepping over will find themselves in spiritual, emotional, and even physical turmoil and disequilibrium. Recall how Zeezrom's wicked ways caused him to have an "exceedingly sore" mind (Alma 15:3, 5).

While the effects of disobedience are not always immediate, they are sure. Seeking after the forbidden fruit always has negative consequences. Carnal pleasure will ultimately give way to pain and sorrow. And the reverse is also true. While the rewards of obedience are not always immediate, they are sure. This is true in temporal as well as spiritual matters.

Years ago a young and talented Latter-day Saint graduated from George Washington University with a degree in mechanical engineering. He immediately turned his back on a promising career and accepted a call to serve a mission in faraway Uruguay. Well-meaning professors and friends tried to dissuade him from his chosen course, suggesting that it would severely harm his budding and promising engineering career. Obeying the voice of the Spirit, the young man spent the next thirty-one months of his life serving the Lord full-time as a missionary.

Upon his return, he was selected to enter the infant Naval Nuclear Program, and he was quickly selected for leadership positions. The effects of his obedience in deciding to disregard the siren voices of those who tried to dissuade him from serving a mission became evident as he quickly rose in leadership and prominence. On one occasion he said, "At a meeting I was sent to direct, I found that one of the professors who had counseled me against going on a mission was in a significantly lesser program position than I. It was a powerful testimony to me of how the Lord blessed me as I put my priorities straight" (*Ensign*, Nov. 1977, 44).

Such was the testimony of a man who has continually made right choices in defining moments and who now serves as one of the the Lord's special witnesses in the Quorum of the Twelve Apostles—Elder Richard G. Scott.

Occasionally, the Lord and His servants patiently persist with one who is reticent to respond to calls to serve. On high school graduation night many years ago, a young man named Ross Workman asked his girlfriend Kaye to marry him. She and her family had been successful in helping him become more active in the Church, but a mission was not in his plans. In fact, he had twice refused the bishop's invitation to serve a mission.

Then came a defining moment. As he was leaving the church parking lot one day following meetings, he was startled to have someone knock on his car window. Ross rolled down the window and was greeted by the face of his stake president. "I've been inspired to ask you one more time to go on a mission," the priesthood leader said. The Spirit was so strong that the young man replied, "I'll go!" His fiancée supported him in the decision, and his life took a new direction. He served faithfully in many callings for more than forty years and then was called to serve as one of the General Authorities of The Church of Jesus Christ of Latter-day Saints (*Church News*, June 16, 2001, 11).

As a result of his obedience to the call of a priesthood leader, Elder Workman is now blessing the lives of countless others through his own priesthood service. What if he had declined that inspired invitation in a church parking lot? How different might have been his life, the lives of his family members, and the lives of those whom he has affected in the past or will yet affect in the future!

There are relatively few whose righteous choices in

public or private defining moments will lead them to positions in the leading councils of the Church or public prominence. However, correct choices should not be governed by expectations of rewards or promises of prestige. Love of God and our fellow beings, with an honest desire to serve them, should be the driving forces behind our desire to be obedient. Each righteous person makes a difference for good in the world regardless of position. There are countless individuals who have made such a difference but whose names will never appear on mortal marquees or in banner headlines. While they may be unknown to the world, they are known to our Father in Heaven.

The importance of obedience is not limited to seemingly defining moments but is also significant in what might be considered minor matters. Recently the Lord's prophet gave counsel on personal matters that without serious consideration might be thought of as inconsequential in terms of their impact on self and others. President Gordon B. Hinckley admonished people to regard their bodies as temples of God (see 1 Corinthians 3:16) and not to deface them with tattoos and piercings (*Ensign*, Nov. 2000, 52; 99). He did not condemn the wearing of earrings for pierced ears by women but said such should be limited to one pair.

Some took offense at this counsel, declaring their independent control over their *own* bodies. "Besides," they complained, "my tattoo or body piercing is not hurting anyone. I'm still a good person." Others, however, obediently responded. One such person was a seventeen-year-old young woman who had recently had her ears pierced a second time. She immediately took out the second pair of earrings and said, "If President Hinckley says we should only wear one set of earrings, that's good enough for me." In commenting on this quick response, one of the Lord's apostles, Elder M. Russell Ballard, said, "Wearing two pair of earrings may or may not have eternal consequences for this young woman, but her willingness to obey the prophet will. And if she will obey him now, on something relatively simple, how much easier it will be to follow him when greater issues are at stake" (*Ensign*, May 2001, 66).

On another occasion, another prophet and president of the Church, Harold B. Lee, counseled priesthood holders to be clean shaven. The wife of one bearded man wrote to President Lee complaining about the dictum, suggesting that her husband was only following the example of Old Testament prophets who wore beards.

In a kind but straightforward manner, President Lee replied to the woman's letter. He reminded her that she had referred to him as "the Lord's prophet" and then asked, "Are you following, in looks, prophets who lived hundreds of years ago? Are you really true to your faith as a member of the Church in failing to look to those who preside in the Church today? Why is it that you want your husband to look like Moses and Jacob, rather than to look like the modern prophets to whom you are expressing allegiance? If you will give this sober thought, your tears will dry, and you'll begin to have some new thoughts" (*Speeches of the Year* [1974] [Provo: BYU Press, 1975], 97–98).

Obedience is displayed in following the *living* prophet, the leader of the Church declared by the Lord to be "the only true and *living* church upon the face of the whole earth" (D&C 1:30; emphasis added). Prophets receive revelation for the needs and protection of the people *today*. Admittedly, in a *living* Church, these current needs will differ from those in days gone by. As President Ezra Taft Benson once put it, the living prophet has "TNT"— *Today's News Today!*

In following the Lord, His prophets, or His undershepherds, such as bishops, it would be well to keep in mind Adam's response to the angel's question about why the first man was offering sacrifices to the Lord. "I know not," replied Adam, "save the Lord commanded me" (Moses 5:6). Centuries later the Prophet of the Restoration, Joseph Smith, made a similar statement when he declared, "I made this my rule: When the Lord commands, do it" (*History of The Church of Jesus Christ of Latter-day Saints*, 7 vols. 2d ed. rev, edited by B. H. Roberts [Salt Lake City: The Church of Jesus Christ of Latter-day Saints, 1932–51], 2:170).

Knowing that whatever God asks us to do is best for us should be sufficient reason to respond obediently (see 2 Nephi 26:24). In contrast to the intent of Heavenly Father and the Savior to lift us to joy is the devil's desire to make us as miserable as he is (see 2 Nephi 2:17, 27).

A simple children's song, based on the words of a prophet, remind us of the rewards of obedience: "Keep the commandments; keep the commandments! / In this there is safety; in this there is peace. / He will send blessings; He will send blessings. / Words of a prophet: Keep the commandments. / In this there is safety and peace" ("Keep the Commandments," *Children's Songbook* [1989], 146–47).

To break, bend, or violate the laws of God or of society in any way places one in spiritual and physical peril. A person may "get away" with breaking the rules for a time, but there will always be a day of reckoning. Consider the case of the football players whose serious violation of team rules negatively affected their entire team and the school they represented. The night before a nationally televised New Year's Day bowl game, these miscreant members of the team engaged in activities they knew to be wrong and which they had promised to avoid. The next day their team was badly beaten, in large measure because some key players were not at their best as a result of disobeying the rules.

Some years later, one of these same football players was in flight training in the military. Thinking he could still bend and break the rules, he cheated his way through the emergency procedures portion of his training. Instead of spending time learning these critical skills, he spent his time on the golf course. When asked how he was going to handle an emergency without being properly trained, he flippantly replied, "I'm never going to [have to] bail out; I am never going to have an emergency." Several months later he suffered the consequences of his disobedience when his plane developed some problems and, because of his lack of preparation, he wasn't able to respond correctly and lost his life in a fiery crash (*Ensign*, May 1990, 40).

In my youth a popular love ballad included the words "little things mean a lot." This same phrase could be applied to choices that may not seem monumental at the time but will later have significant consequences. Certainly the seemingly small choices made by the football player–pilot just described had such results. Elder Joseph B. Wirthlin once admonished, "Let us pay heed to the 'small things' that make all the difference" (*Ensign*, May 1996, 34).

Many years ago a Latter-day Saint athlete named Creed Haymond was a star runner and captain of the track team at the University of Pennsylvania. His track coach would later coach several Olympic teams. The night before an Inter-Collegiate Association track meet, the coach instructed each team member to drink some sherry wine, which was wrongly considered to be a good tonic for muscles at the time.

While he did not want to be disobedient to the coach, Creed felt a higher responsibility to be obedient to his religious beliefs and to God. He therefore refused to drink the proffered wine in spite of the urging of his coach, who pleaded, "Remember, Creed, you're the captain of the team and our best point winner. Fourteen thousand students are looking to you personally to win this meet. If you fail us, we'll lose. I ought to know what is good for you." Creed was steadfast in his resolve to remain true to his principles.

The next day the coach arrived early in Creed's room to inquire about his health. He informed the Latter-day Saint runner that the rest of the team had taken ill. "I don't know what's the matter with them," the coach said. "Maybe," replied Creed, "it's the tonic you gave them." As a result of this turn of events, Creed Haymond was the only member of the team who was able to perform well in the meet that day. He won the 100-yard dash, even after a mishap at the start when his foot slipped, and he won the 200-yard dash in record time. His obedience in a seemingly small thing paid large dividends (*Improvement Era*, Oct. 1928, 1001–7).

The violation of seemingly small rules and regulations can lead to large and disastrous results. Elder Joseph B. Wirthlin gave the analogy of careless campers who had not properly extinguished a campfire. In truth they might even have rationalized their actions by saying, "It was *almost* out!"

"The first deviation toward moral breakdown in a man or woman is similar to a spark that ignites a devastating forest fire. On a hot, windy summer day this year in Midway, Utah, embers from a small campground fire were fanned into a raging forest fire that soon swept over the entire mountainside. Before the flames were brought under control, the lives of two outstanding members of the Church were lost. The roaring fire had destroyed the beautiful autumn foliage, plus eighteen homes. We risk similar damage to our moral integrity when we let our guard down for even one brief moment. The spark of an evil thought can enter our mind that could ignite and destroy the moral fiber of our soul" (*Ensign*, Nov. 1990, 65).

President Gordon B. Hinckley has wisely counseled, "I should like to emphasize the importance of watching the little things in our lives. . . . Small acts of dishonesty, small acts of an immoral nature, small outbursts of anger can grow into great and terrible things" (*Ensign*, May 1984, 81).

Chapter 11

ALMOST PERSUADED

❖ ❖ ❖ ❖ ❖ ❖ ❖ ❖ ❖ ❖

"Almost thou persuadest me to be a Christian" (Acts 26:28).

With these momentous words, King Agrippa momentarily teetered on the threshold of testimony, but, rejecting the promptings of the Spirit, he turned his back on the apostolic witness borne by Paul. Agrippa *almost* became a follower of Jesus Christ with all of a follower's eternal blessings. He almost accepted the saving ordinances of the gospel. He almost changed his life for the better. He almost became a candidate for the celestial kingdom.

How often in history have men or women faced defining moments for goodness and greatness and *almost* made the right decisions?

Perhaps Pilate *almost* became a man of principle when he "marvelled greatly" in the presence of the Prince of Peace, the true King of kings (see Matthew 27:11–14). Notwithstanding the impression made on him by Jesus, Pilate sought the political safety and friendship of the wicked Herod Antipas and the errant Sanhedrin rather than to save the sinless Son of God.

Succumbing to social pressure, he vainly sought to wash his hands of the matter. Yet, as Elder Neal A. Maxwell has so well stated, "Pilate's hands were never dirtier than just after he had washed them" (in Conference Report, Oct. 1974, 16).

Assistance from Pilate might not have spared the Savior or delayed His date with death—for divine decree declared the Atonement an essential part of the plan. Yet Pilate's preference for the pleasure of the crowd rather than the peace of principle left lasting scars on his soul. In a defining moment of history he branded himself as a less than momentous man.

While most of us will not face situations of such magnitude and public visibility, we all confront challenges to our characters that have eternal consequences. Each day we must make choices that are either right or wrong. While occasionally it may be difficult to discern a clear-cut choice between the two, it is important not to rationalize to ourselves that accepting so-called *gray* areas, or sampling a *piece* of forbidden fruit *just once*, won't really matter.

Elder Dean L. Larsen has cautioned, "Too frequently Latter-day Saints of all ages yield to the temptation to explore and sample forbidden things of the world. Often this is not done with the intent to embrace these things permanently, but with the knowing decision to indulge in them momentarily, as though they hold a value of some kind too important or too exciting to pass by. While some recover from these excursions, an increasingly large number of tragedies occur that bring a blight and a despair into many lives" (Conference Report, Oct. 1981, 37).

"A little sin will not stay little," noted Elder ElRay L. Christiansen (Conference Report, Oct. 1974, 29).

Consider the case of King Saul, who was commanded

by the Lord to destroy the wicked Amalekites and *all* that they possessed. Although Saul and his people commenced to carry out the commandment of the Lord, they failed to follow it completely. Greed clouded their vision, and they looked with lust upon the livestock they had been commanded to destroy and spared "the best . . . and would not utterly destroy them" (1 Samuel 15:9).

When confronted by the prophet Samuel, Saul sought to rationalize his rejection of God's counsel. His explanation was that the people intended to sacrifice the animals to the Lord. Samuel rebuked the errant king by declaring, "Hath the Lord as great delight in burnt offerings and sacrifices, as in obeying the voice of the Lord? Behold, to obey is better than sacrifice" (1 Samuel 15:22).

Saul's slide to sin came through disobedience. He commenced his career as king with a character described as "choice . . . and there was not among the children of Israel a goodlier person than he" (1 Samuel 9:2). Yet the promise of youth was erased through a series of wrong choices. His uncontrolled self-will ultimately led him to a rejection by God and death by his own suicidal sword (see 1 Samuel 28:6, 15; 31:4).

Sometimes we face decisions that on the surface do not appear to be evil. We may not be deliberately seeking sin but merely avoiding the pursuit of a better path. However, the New Testament reminds us that "to him that knoweth to do good, and doeth it not, to him it is sin" (James 4:17). Thus, when we settle for less than the best, we suffer negative consequences.

"There came one running, and kneeled to [Jesus], and

asked him, Good Master, what shall I do that I may inherit eternal life?" Do you recall the Savior's response? He reiterated the basic commandments. The man responded that he had observed these things from the time of his youth.

"Then Jesus beholding him loved him, and said unto him, *One thing thou lackest.*" He asked him to sell all he possessed, give the proceeds to the poor, and follow him.

This was too much of a sacrifice, "for he had great possessions." Although he grieved, the man nevertheless rejected the Redeemer's invitation to serve (see Mark 10:17–22; emphasis added).

We do not know the name of this man or what became of him. Had he accepted the challenge to sacrifice and serve, he might have been one of the great ones of the kingdom. That he was not an evil man is evident. He observed the commandments. Yet he *lacked one thing.*

A great lesson should be learned from this experience. There should be *no* exclusions in our willingness to serve and sacrifice. How often are we *lacking one thing* when an opportunity for sacrifice or service arises?

Remember that a true follower of Christ is completely committed. Such a one does not place exclusion clauses in his contract with God. His song is *not,* "I'll go where you want me to go, dear Lord, I'll say what you want me to say, I'll be what you want me to be, *but . . .*"

The pages of history are filled with the names of those who were less than momentous when it really mattered. Different choices on their parts could have changed the course of history. There are also numberless, nameless men and women whose potential was never reached and who remain unknown because they made the wrong decisions during defining moments.

Ultimately, whether our names and deeds are penned in the pages of history does not really matter. What does matter is how we react when faced with critical choices. In reality there are no minor choices, for each choice we make leads to consequences that are stamped on our character. Thus, all choices are critical! Each moment matters!

Chapter 12

FOLLOW THE
PROMPTINGS

❖ ❖ ❖ ❖ ❖ ❖ ❖ ❖ ❖

"For they that are wise and have received the truth, and have taken the Holy Spirit for their guide . . . have not been deceived" (D&C 45:57).

Deception is a key tool of the devil. He will try to muddy the waters of the mind so that decision-making becomes more difficult. Confusion is his ally.

The deceiver was successful in leading one-third of our Heavenly Father's spirit children in making the wrong choice (see D&C 29:36–37). The door to eternal progression is forever closed to these followers of the master fool. Since the time of his open rebellion in our pre-earthly home, Satan has continued to use deception in seeking to lure the remaining two-thirds of God's children to foolishly follow him by making wrong choices.

The devil desperately desires to have each of us become as foolish and miserable as he is. The ancient prophet Nephi warned that Satan "seeketh that all men might be miserable like unto himself" (2 Nephi 2:27).

Reflect on times when you have made wrong choices. Do you recall the misery you felt on such occasions? Contrast these feelings with the joy that bathed your being when you followed proper paths.

Providentially, God has given a gift to His children that can help them avoid the devil's deceptions: "The

Spirit of Christ is given to every man, that he may know good from evil; wherefore, I show unto you the way to judge; for every thing which inviteth to do good, and to persuade to believe in Christ, is sent forth by the power and gift of Christ; wherefore ye may know with a perfect knowledge it is of God.

"But whatsoever thing persuadeth men to do evil, and believe not in Christ, and deny him, and serve not God, then ye may know with a perfect knowledge it is of the devil; for after this manner doth the devil work, for he persuadeth no man to do good, no, not one; neither do his angels; neither do they who subject themselves unto him. . . .

"Search diligently in the light of Christ; . . . lay hold upon every good thing" (Moroni 7:16–17, 19).

In addition to the Light of Christ, God has given another gift to those who accept His gospel and receive the saving ordinances thereof. The gift of the Holy Ghost—the right to the constant companionship of this holy member of the Godhead—is conferred on each baptized member of The Church of Jesus Christ of Latter-day Saints. The gift, however, is contingent on our faithfulness, for the Spirit will not remain in the presence of evil.

The promptings of the Spirit are often referred to as "the still, small voice" (see 1 Kings 19:11–12; D&C 85:6). One who described his experience with this form of revelation said, "The voice of the Lord came into my mind" (Enos 1:10).

Elder Boyd K. Packer has observed, "There is a spiritual beam, with a constant signal. If you know how to pray and how to listen, spiritually listen, you may move through life, through clear weather, through storms, through wars, through peace, and be all right." ("Prayers and Answers," *Ensign*, Nov. 1979, 21).

During World War II, Elder Packer was flying as a co-pilot on a B-17 in the South Pacific. For some reason, the plane got off course, and the navigator was unable to determine their location. The radios were out, and so the men began flying a "square search." This was a pattern used to keep track of what territory they had been covering so that the aircraft was not flying over an area that had previously been covered.

The plane was dangerously low on fuel, and the likelihood of their having to ditch in the treacherous ocean waters below them became more real by the minute. As they neared the end of one pattern run, the other pilot proposed that they turn. "Hold it just a minute," said Elder Packer. He did not know why he made the suggestion, but it turned out to be providential, for suddenly they could see a long line of white waves below them in the water. This was a sign that land was nearby. With a prayer in their hearts, they intuitively followed the flight pattern they thought best and in a few minutes landed safely on a small Pacific island. As they landed and were taxiing down the runway, one by one the engines turned off. They were out of gas!

"During the last hour of that flight," reflected Elder Packer, "when I sat there wondering if we would or if we wouldn't make it, my patriarchal blessing kept coming to my mind. It said, 'You will be warned of danger, and if you heed those warnings you will be privileged to return to your loved ones.' I thought, 'Well, I've tried.' I sat there thinking, 'The gospel's true and what else matters? That prophetic declaration will see us safely through this, and if it doesn't, we're in the hands of the Lord now.'" ("Follow the Rule," *1977 Devotional Speeches of the Year* [Provo: BYU Press, 1978], 23).

This spiritual beam to which Elder Packer responded, this still, small voice—the prompting of the Spirit—has been responsible for saving the temporal and the spiritual lives of many throughout history.

Not many years ago a family went on vacation. Upon arriving at the motel, the children quickly got into their swimming suits and were in the swimming pool before the car was unloaded. As the father passed the pool, he saw a sign that struck him with great force: Do Not Leave Children Unattended. He had seen similar signs on other occasions, but this time it was different. Although he felt a need to finish unloading the car, there was a greater prompting that compelled him to remain at the pool. In a matter of minutes, his decision to stay at the pool was validated; one of his daughters was soon "in deep water, and deep trouble, and struggling for help."

How much better was the water-drenched clothing of the father—who dove in to save his daughter's life—than the tear-stained clothes he might have worn had he not heeded the promptings of the Spirit! (see James M. Paramore, in Conference Report, Apr. 1983, 36).

One who developed a finely honed spiritual ear was

the man who became the fourth president of The Church of Jesus Christ of Latter-day Saints, Wilford Woodruff.

In 1848 he was traveling with his family on an assignment from the First Presidency. One night he and his wife and one child were sleeping in their wagon when a voice said to him, "Get up, and move your carriage." Elder Woodruff described the voice as "the still, small voice of the Spirit of God—the Holy Ghost."

He did not hesitate to obey. Awakening his wife, he told her that he must move the carriage. When she asked why, he admitted he did not know the *reason* for the action but he did *recognize the source* of the warning. After moving the carriage, he was warned by the Spirit to move his mules. They were tied to an oak tree some distance from the carriage. Once again, he was unquestioning in his response.

Thirty minutes later, a whirlwind tore through the area, uprooting the tree to which his mules had been tied, dragging it about one hundred yards and leaving it resting on the spot where his carriage had originally stood. The circumference of the tree measured over five feet. If Elder Woodruff had not obeyed the Spirit, death could have resulted to both his family and his animals (see George C. Lambert, *Gems of Reminiscence* [1915], 92–93).

What a great example for all to consider. We may not always know the reason for the Spirit's promptings, but physical and spiritual safety will be the result of obedience.

On another occasion Wilford Woodruff was warned by the Spirit to avoid taking a company of Church members on board a steamer. More than a hundred lives were saved on that occasion because he listened *and* obeyed. In later years he was to say, "I never disobeyed that Spirit but once in my life; I did it then through the urgency of other persons, and it nearly cost me my life" (Preston Nibley, *Faith Promoting Stories* [Salt Lake City: Deseret Book, 1943], 24–26).

Promptings from the Spirit do not always involve life-threatening situations. Occasionally they come as gentle reminders to render a good deed or to lift another's sagging spirit. Such a simple thing as a telephone call, a brief letter, or even a short visit might make a real difference in another's life. We need not wait for a personalized invitation to reach out to another, for we have been counseled to "always abound in good works" (Alma 7:24) and to "do many [good] things" of our own accord (D&C 58:27). Who knows what far-reaching effect even a simple act of kindness on our part may have on the life of another?

One of the greatest opportunities to render service is in sharing the gospel with others through missionary work. The Spirit often whispers quiet promptings that lead to conversions to the truth. Elder Joseph B. Wirthlin related the following example.

A new Elder in Italy, Gary D. Shaw, discovered early in his mission that the Lord would help those who were willing to listen to His promptings. The missionary had been in the mission field for only two weeks when his senior companion became ill and the two had to remain in their apartment for the day. The junior companion was "moved by the Spirit and had a great desire to talk to someone about the gospel, so he picked up the phone book in which more than *three million names* were listed. He chose three. There was no response to the first call. To the second, a woman answered and informed Elder Shaw that she wasn't at all interested, and to make matters worse, declared that she couldn't understand his poor Italian and atrocious mode of speech. On the third try, a man answered. Elder Shaw introduced himself and received a warm response. The man said his name was Mabiglia and that he would gladly receive the Elders. This he did. The appointment made so miraculously turned into a spiritually uplifting and inspiring occasion. . . . The man contacted by telephone was baptized, and Brother Mabiglia is [in 1975] serving in the presidency of the Naples Branch" (Conference Report, Oct. 1975, 156).

Because he was unwilling to "take the day off," and because his heart was right before the Lord, the young missionary heard the prompting of the Spirit. He was not discouraged by the harsh treatment of the woman who belittled his initial efforts but, like Alma after his rejection by the people of Ammonihah, continued his ministry and found the one man to hear his message (see Alma 8).

At times we are prompted by the Spirit to do things almost unknowingly. The inspiration of a moment that mattered may not become apparent until later.

Many years ago a father was quietly reading in his living room. Suddenly, without an audible word being spoken by anyone, he bolted from the chair and raced out of the house and into the orchard. He knew no rational reason for his behavior, only that the Spirit had prompted him to get outside quickly. He observed a riderless horse running wildly through the orchard, with the loose reins of a harness flying in the wind. The father ran to the horse, grabbed the reins, and soon had the shaking animal under control. Only then did he notice the small boy hanging on one side of the horse with his foot caught in the stirrup.

Oscar W. McConkie had responded to the promptings of the Spirit and saved the life of his young son, Bruce. Little did either realize that this boy would one day grow to be a mighty mouthpiece of God, serving as a General Authority of God's Church for thirty-nine years (see "Response to Impulse Saves Small Boy," *Church News*, July 31, 1965, C-16).

Less dramatic than the story of the runaway horse, but just as important, was the experience of a teacher who quietly responded to spiritual promptings.

"One evening . . . a faithful and wonderful Mutual teacher of high school age girls stood to present a carefully prepared lesson when suddenly she was prompted to forego the regular lesson and discuss the tragedy of immorality. About halfway through the lesson, impatient horn-honking was heard from the church parking lot. Finally it stopped, and the car with its youthful male occupant sped away. Following the inspirational discussion in the classroom, one tearful but grateful young lady lingered after the others had departed to confide in her leader that the honking had been for her. Then she said: 'I had decided that tonight was going to be the biggest night of my life, and that horn toot was the signal that all the arrangements were complete, and he was waiting. What you said and how you said it has saved me from the most serious mistake of my life, and I shall never forget it'" (Robert L. Simpson, in Conference Report, Apr. 1968, 117).

It is interesting how the young girl really did make it the "biggest night of her life," for in this defining moment that mattered so much, she avoided a tragedy that would have plagued her the rest of her life. How important it was that her leader was in tune with and obedient to the promptings of the Spirit.

Spiritual promptings do not always occur unsolicited. Many come as a direct result of prayerful pleadings. If we are in tune with the Spirit, there will even be occasions when we become the source of an answer to another's prayers.

President Spencer W. Kimball once noted that "God does notice us, and he watches over us. But it is usually through another person that he meets our needs" ("Small Acts of Service," *Ensign*, Dec. 1974, 5).

Sister Sara (Mrs. N. Eldon) Tanner once related an intriguing story about her nephew. He, his wife, and six children lived in an area where he served as a counselor in the stake presidency. Late one afternoon he took his two eldest children with him to a church function. His wife remained at home with the four younger children.

While attending his meeting, the man was suddenly prompted by the Spirit to return home immediately. He left the meeting abruptly. He did not even stop to get his two children but drove directly home. He entered the home and was immediately confronted by two men with guns. His four children were bound and gagged, and his wife and her mother were seated in sheer terror on the couch.

The husband's arrival home had been the direct result of his wife's silent prayers to the Lord. She had pleaded that her husband would be prompted to come home. The men knocked the husband around but he did not retaliate, even though he was a large, athletic man.

The men became frightened of a two-way radio on the husband's belt that he carried to keep him in contact with his office. Fearing that their presence had been discovered by the police through the paging device, the burglars fled.

The police identified the intruders as two well-known burglars and molesters, whose usual approach was to rob and then rape the victims. Any who had tried to resist them were badly beaten.

In a moment that mattered, a woman was prayerful and a man was in tune with the promptings of the Spirit. As a result, a family was saved from severe harm (see Helsinki Area Conference Report, Aug. 2–3, 1976, 10–11).

Prayer and the promptings of the Spirit can be the means of removing what appear to be insurmountable obstacles. Consider the experience of President Ezra Taft Benson while a member of the Quorum of the Twelve Apostles. He had been sent to war-torn Europe following World War II to reestablish the missions of the Church and to set up a program for the distribution of welfare supplies. One of the first military men he needed to see in order to get permission for the program was the commander of American forces stationed in Europe.

Elder Benson and his traveling companion flew to the general's headquarters in Frankfurt, Germany, and sought an appointment with the man. They were met by the appointment secretary, who said, "Gentlemen, there will be no opportunity for you to see the general for at least three days. He's very busy and his calendar is filled up with appointments."

Elder Benson explained that they could not wait three days and were due in Berlin the following day, but he did not prevail.

"We left the building," said Elder Benson, "went out to our car, removed our hats, and united in prayer. We then went back into the building and found a different officer at the appointment post. In less than fifteen minutes we were in the presence of the general" (Conference Report, Apr. 1977, 46).

Because he followed the prompting to pray—for "the Spirit . . . teacheth a man to pray" (2 Nephi 32:8)—Elder Benson was successful in his assignment. Many lives were blessed because someone prayed and the Spirit opened the doors for success.

If we will pray rather than panic during defining moments that matter, we will experience the soothing calmness of the Spirit and will be directed to take the right course of action.

Several years ago, Bishop H. Burke Peterson was on an assignment in Europe. He had been fighting the flu and had an extremely sore throat. After landing at the airport in Frankfurt, Germany, he checked into the airport hotel to get some much-needed rest. Before retiring to his bed, he went to the hotel pharmacy and purchased some throat disinfectant to ease his discomfort.

The medication came in a push-button can that dispensed its healing properties through a finger-length piece of plastic tubing that the patient was supposed to stick into the throat.

Bishop Peterson returned to his room and began to spray his throat. "But," he said, "the plastic tube came loose and drove itself down my throat and into my chest. I couldn't feel it, but I knew there was a three-inch piece of plastic somewhere, and I didn't know what to do. I coughed. I did all that I could to get rid of it. Then I began to worry—not that I would die, for I knew that I wasn't near death—but because I knew that there were people waiting for me in various countries where I was to be going for the next three weeks, and I knew that if something didn't happen right away I would end up in the hospital to have the plastic pipe removed surgically. So I needed an immediate answer. I needed an immediate response. I knelt at my bed, and I told the Lord that I had no place to go, that I didn't speak the language, that I didn't know a doctor, that I didn't know anyone, and that there were people waiting for me. And I asked Him to please remove this tubing. I got up from praying, and in two seconds [I coughed again and] it came out of my throat."

As he spoke about this experience, Bishop Peterson noted:

"The pattern of our lives determines our eligibility to receive the promptings of the Spirit and to hear the answers to our prayers. Again, let there be no misunderstanding.

Heavenly Father does answer our prayers, but often we aren't prepared to hear Him. Some prayers are not answered immediately, and that's where we may become discouraged. Some are answered immediately" ("Prayer: Try Again," *1980 Devotional Speeches of the Year* [Provo: BYU Press, 1981], 35).

One of the things that often impedes our ability to listen to the promptings of the Spirit is fear. Fear is incompatible with faith. The Apostle Paul reminded us that "God hath not given us the spirit of fear; but of power, and of love, and of a sound mind" (2 Timothy 1:7).

Years ago a young missionary in Australia went to visit the spectacular Jenolan Caves. As he walked through these wonders of nature on a guided tour, the guide said, "If some of you will get out and stand on that rock over there and sing a song, it will demonstrate the capacity of this cave."

The Spirit whispered to the missionary to step forward and sing the hymn, "O My Father," but the Elder hesitated and the crowd moved on. The opportunity was lost. What heart might have been touched by the inspired words of that special hymn if the young man had responded to the Spirit?

David O. McKay, the ninth President of The Church of Jesus Christ of Latter-day Saints, once advised, "Never fail to respond to the whisperings of the Spirit. Live so you can receive it, and then have the courage to do as it instructs" (as quoted by Marion G. Romney in Conference Report, Apr. 1975, 110).

Obedience is a key to receiving answers to prayers and to being in tune with the promptings of the Spirit. Many years ago, a young missionary by the name of Gordon B. Hinckley served in the European Mission Office under a member of the Quorum of the Twelve Apostles, Elder Joseph F. Merrill. One day President Merrill called the young missionary into his office and asked him to go visit the publisher of a "snide and ugly" book that purported to be a history of Mormonism. Elder Hinckley was asked to protest the publication.

The young missionary was fearful but obedient. "I went to my room," he said, "and felt . . . as I think Moses must have felt when the Lord asked him to go and see Pharaoh. I offered a prayer. My stomach was churning as I [went] to the . . . office of the [publisher] and presented my card to the receptionist. She took it and went into the inner office and returned to say that Mr. Skeffington was too busy to see me. I replied that I had come five thousand miles and that I would wait. During the next hour she made two or three trips to his office, then finally invited me in. I shall never forget the picture when I entered. He was smoking a long cigar with a look that seemed to say, 'Don't bother me.'

"I held in my hand the reviews. I do not know what I said after that. Another power seemed to be speaking through me. At first he was defensive and even belligerent. Then he began to soften. He concluded by promising to do something. Within an hour word went out to every book dealer in England to return the books to the publisher. At great expense he printed and inserted in the front of each volume a statement to the effect that the book was not to be considered as history, but only as fiction, and that no offense was intended against the respected Mormon people. . . .

"I came to know that when we try in faith to walk in obedience to the requests of the priesthood, the Lord opens the way, even when there appears to be no way" (Conference Report, Oct. 1971, 161).

This obedient missionary experienced the truthfulness of Nephi's prophetic proclamation: "I will go and do the things which the Lord hath commanded [either directly or through my priesthood leaders], for I know that the Lord giveth no commandments unto the children of men, save he shall prepare a way for them that they may accomplish the thing which he commandeth them" (1 Nephi 3:7).

Pausing for prayer before making a decision or taking action can open the door to the whisperings of the Spirit, which might otherwise be missed.

Elder F. Enzio Busche described an experience he had because he paused for prayer and listened to the accompanying promptings of the Spirit.

"One day when circumstances made it necessary for me to be at home at an unusual time," he related, "I witnessed from another room how our eleven-year-old son, just returning from school, was directing ugly words towards his younger sister. They were words that offended me—words that I had never thought our son would use. My first natural reaction in my anger was to get up and go after him. Fortunately, I had to walk across the room and open a door before I could reach him, and I remember in those few seconds I *fervently prayed* to my Heavenly Father to help me handle the situation. Peace came over me. I was no longer angry."

A simple prayer turned what could have been an ugly confrontation into a teaching moment. "The Spirit shall be given unto you by the prayer of faith; and if ye receive not the Spirit ye shall not teach" (D&C 42:14).

Prepared by the Spirit to teach, Elder Busche approached his son in a spirit of love rather than anger. Their hearts were knit together as they talked. The son expressed his sorrow over the incident with his sister, and the two "ended up crying together, hugging each other in love and finally in joy. What could have been a disastrous confrontation between father and son," recounted Elder Busche, "became, through the help from the powers above, one of the most beautiful experiences of our relationship that we both have never forgotten" ("Love Is the Power That Will Cure the Family," *Ensign*, May 1982, 70; emphasis added).

Occasionally promptings from the Spirit turn us to fervent prayer in behalf of one whom we feel is in need of a special blessing. Numerous accounts have been related through the years of how individuals who were sensitive to the Spirit sought the spiritual or physical safety of a loved one through the medium of prayer. Sometimes these promptings came as gentle breezes blowing through the recesses of the mind, while on other occasions the promptings have come with great force, literally driving the recipients to their knees.

Some years ago, three young boys found themselves in difficulty as they tried to maneuver a small craft down a rapidly running river. The boat was suddenly struck by a large tree that was floating down the swiftly moving water, and the craft capsized. One of the boys was thrown onto the safety of a sandbar; another clung tenaciously to the overturned boat; but the third, a boy named John, fell into deep water and became entangled in the roots and branches of the floating tree.

His struggle to free himself left him exhausted, and the last thing he remembered, before losing consciousness, was feeling his fingers slip from the muddy bank into which he had desperately dug them.

At this same moment, more than fifty miles away in another city, John's father suddenly had a strong impression that he should pray for the safety of his son. Although he did not know the nature of his son's trouble, the father prayerfully petitioned the Lord to intercede in the boy's behalf and save him from whatever danger was threatening his life.

The prayer was answered and John was saved. When he regained consciousness, he found himself standing alone on the bank of the river, about ten feet from where he had felt himself slipping away into what appeared to be a watery grave (see "Drowning Boy Miraculously Saved for Service to Church," *Church News*, Apr. 22, 1961, C16).

When no mortal help is available, unseen but very real help is available from the other side of the veil. But would that help have been as readily available to John if his father had not been responsive to the promptings of the Spirit in a moment that really mattered?

We should never postpone following the promptings of

the Spirit. To ignore a spiritual prompting is to invite disaster, despair, and disappointment.

In defining moments that matter so very much seek the promptings of the Spirit.

Pause for prayer!

Chapter 13

THE POWER
OF PRAYER

❖ ❖ ❖ ❖ ❖ ❖ ❖ ❖ ❖ ❖ ❖

A few years ago a giant 747 jetliner was flying over the Pacific Ocean when suddenly it sustained a gigantic tear in its side. Nine passengers were instantly hurled to their deaths, and the terrified remaining passengers clung tightly to their seats, hoping their seat belts and seats would remain in place. Through the skillful flying of Captain David Cronin, the plane was able to land in Hawaii without further loss of life.

Asked how he was able to fly the crippled aircraft and save the lives of so many, the pilot replied, "I prayed, then went to work!" In a moment of crisis that mattered so much to the crew and passengers on that ill-fated aircraft, the captain turned to the divine Source for much-needed help. *Then* he went to work to solve the problem. This joint partnership between God and man in resolving problems was expressed by President Ezra Taft Benson: "*After making a request through prayer, we have a responsibility to assist in its being granted*" (*Ensign*, May 1977, 33).

How often do we turn *first* to our Father in Heaven for help when faced with a problem? Are we taking advantage of the offer of strength and support He so willingly extends to us, or are we content to rely solely upon our own talents and resources? Each of us would do well to follow the example of faithful Nephi, who said, "I will not put my trust in the arm of flesh" (2 Nephi 4:34).

Our Father in Heaven wants to hear from us because we are His children. He desires to bless us. "Did he ask us to pray because he wants us to bow down and worship him?" asked President Joseph Fielding Smith. "Is that the main reason? I don't think it is. . . . The Lord can get along without our prayers. His work will go on just the same, whether we pray or whether we do not. He knows the end from the beginning. . . . Prayer is something that *we* need, not that the Lord needs. . . . Our prayers are uttered more for our sakes, to build us up and give us strength and courage, and to increase our faith in him" (*Improvement Era*, June 1968, 40).

There is great power in prayer. There is great peace in knowing that a divine ear is listening and that strength and solutions are forthcoming.

Not all problems will be resolved—at least in the manner we anticipate—for God allows agency to be exercised and lessons to be learned, including patience and long-suffering.

Consider, for example, the circumstances of those marvelous missionaries, the sons of Mosiah. They forsook the comforts of life, including the chance to succeed their father as the king, to take a fourteen-year ministry among a hostile people. They were specifically admonished to "be patient in long-suffering and afflictions" (Alma 17:11). Their success was won amid numerous trials and difficulties, but they were strengthened because, among other things, "they had given themselves to much prayer" (Alma 17:3).

Another classic example of the power of prayer is found in the Book of Mormon account of the faithful colony of Alma the elder. These good people were brought into bondage by an army of Lamanites who broke a promise of freedom for the colony if Alma would show them the way out of the wilderness. The little colony was then subjected to being ruled by wicked men who mistreated them and commanded them not to pray under penalty of death (see Mosiah 23–24).

Suppose you were in such a situation where vocal or public prayer was forbidden, or perhaps out of place? What would you do?

The faithful people under Alma's leadership determined to pray in their hearts. I believe those prayers were not only for relief from their oppression but also an expression of continued gratitude for the gospel that had so changed their lives. The Lord answered their prayers in an interesting manner. He allowed them to remain in bondage for a time, trying "their patience and their faith" (Mosiah 23:21). However, He lightened the weight of the burdens that had been placed upon them; "yea, the Lord did strengthen them that they could bear up their burdens with ease" (Mosiah 24:15).

In time the people were led out of bondage. But in the intervening time they leaned upon the spiritual and physical strength they received from Him who would later declare, "Come unto me, all ye that labour and are heavy laden, and I will give you rest. . . . For my yoke is easy, and my burden is light" (Matthew 11:28, 30).

Sickness, sorrow, whatever one's suffering or difficulty may be, the divine promise is sure: the Lord will lift that burden. I had a particularly meaningful experience in having a burden lifted while serving as a mission president in the Netherlands and Belgium.

A mission president and his wife grow very close to the missionaries with whom they serve. It is as if their family has expanded, being added to by the scores of young men and women who come under their care. The president and his wife pray fervently in behalf of these new members of the family, and they are humbled to know that the missionaries, and their families, in turn are praying for them. And there are others who pray for those mission presidents and their families.

Those prayers were particularly comforting during a time of great sorrow in our mission. Tragedy struck, and the life of one of our missionary sons was taken. The burden we had to bear was heavy, and the depth of our personal pain and sorrow ran deep. We were not alone in that suffering, for the death of one of their fellow laborers also affected the missionaries. Yet through it all came a spiritual strength and easing of the burden we bore that cannot be adequately described.

"The Brethren of the First Presidency and Quorum of the Twelve Apostles are praying for you," said Elder Gene R. Cook of the Seventy. "They have prayed for you in the temple," he added. These comforting words and the sure knowledge that the prayers of the Lord's anointed were being offered in our behalf gave us the strength to deal with a tragedy that otherwise might have devastated us. I can personally testify of the absolute power of prayers of faith being offered in one's behalf.

In moments of crisis, turn to the Lord for strength and invite others to join you in that effort. It is not mere rhetoric when bishops, other priesthood leaders, and even speakers in church meetings invite us to pray for them.

When Elder John H. Groberg arrived in his field of labor as a young missionary to the South Pacific, he was immediately faced with a challenging situation. The immigration officials in Fiji would not allow him off the boat. The problem was compounded because the captain would not allow him to stay on the boat, and the young elder was essentially stuck in "no-man's-land" on the gangplank between the ship and the shore. After considerable arguing, he was placed in the "not-too-friendly" hands of customs officials.

He was supposed to have been met at the dock by two missionaries who were to put him on another boat to Tonga, but the missionaries did not show up, and Elder Groberg found himself in a customs shed. As the hours passed, the tired, hungry, and frightened missionary prayed for help. Day turned to dusk, and once again the forlorn missionary closed his eyes in fervent prayer.

He said, "Suddenly I felt almost transported. I didn't see anything or hear anything, in a physical sense; but, in a more real way, I saw a family in far-off Idaho kneeling together in prayer; and I heard my mother, acting as mouth, say as clearly as anything can be heard, 'And bless John on his mission.'"

Elder Groberg later testified of the power that came to him at this critical moment. "As that faithful family called down the powers of heaven to bless their missionary son in a way they could not physically do, I testify that the powers of heaven did come down, and they lifted me up and, in a spiritual way, allowed me, for a brief moment, to once again join that family circle in prayer. I was one with them. I was literally swallowed up in the love and concern of a faithful family and sensed for a moment what being taken into Abraham's bosom may be like. (See Luke 16:22.) I was given to understand also that there are other circles of love and concern unbounded by time or space to which we all belong and from which we can draw strength. God does not leave us entirely alone—ever!" (*Ensign*, May 1982, 51–52).

There was a happy ending to Elder Groberg's dilemma. On his way home from work, a customs official spotted two young men with white shirts and ties and told them of the other young man dressed in a white shirt and tie. Evidently they had not received the telegram informing them of the missionary's arrival. Within a short time the problem was resolved as prayers were answered.

The power of prayer in behalf of family members is illustrated in the miraculous change of life of Alma the younger and the four sons of Mosiah. These youths had taken a rebellious path that brought great sorrow to their faithful fathers, both of whom were righteous leaders in the community. While on one of their wicked escapades, the five young men were rebuked by an angel of God, who called them to repentance.

Speaking specifically of Alma the younger's father, the angel said, "He has prayed with much faith concerning thee" (Mosiah 27:14).

Not all parental prayers are answered with visitations from heavenly messengers. Sometimes those prayers are answered in the form of mortal messengers. I know of a faithful father and mother who constantly pray that faithful friends will come into the life of their wandering and much-loved child. We never know when our own act of reaching out in an act of charity or just plain friendliness may be the answer to another's prayers.

Many years ago Newton Hall and his family were in dire straits. His family was without food, and there didn't seem to be any solution to their situation. It was a time of impoverishment for many families, and the Halls had been unsuccessful in their efforts to obtain relief or assistance. He went alone to a wooded area and desperately pleaded in solemn prayer for help. Shortly thereafter there came a knock at his door. There stood Joseph Millett with a sack of flour in his arms. He had been told by his children that the Halls were out of food.

"Brother Hall," the visitor asked, "are you out of flour?"

The sad answer: "We have none."

"Well," replied Brother Millett, "there is some in that sack. I have divided what I had and it is yours."

The grateful recipient of this generous gift thanked his benefactor and explained that he had tried to get help from others without success. When he told Brother Millett of his prayerful pleadings to the Lord, the man responded that if his gift was the result of a prayer that it need not be paid back.

That evening Joseph Millett recorded the following entry in his journal: "You can't tell me how good it made me feel to know that the Lord knew there was such a person as Joseph Millett" (Diary of Joseph Millett, holograph, Archives of The Church of Jesus Christ of Latter-day Saints, Salt Lake City; see also *Ensign*, May 1980, 63).

Yes, our Father in Heaven often answers prayers through the acts of love and service of His children on this earth. One never knows when he or she might be the Lord's answer to another's prayerful pleadings for help.

I have personally witnessed this miracle time and again as I have served in priesthood callings over the years. Numerous are the occasions when almost imperceptibly I have been prompted to visit or call someone at a moment that really mattered in their lives. This personal experience of mine has been repeated untold times by other priesthood and auxiliary leaders as well as spiritually sensitive individuals without any particular church calling.

One evening during dinner, a mother suddenly jumped to her feet and announced that she needed to leave for a few minutes. As she went out the door, the husband and children wondered what errand of mercy she was attending to on this occasion, for this was not a new experience for them. The woman was known for her acts of love and kindness in behalf of others.

She drove to the home of a neighbor and knocked on the door. The woman who opened the door appeared red-eyed and in distress. Upon inviting her visitor in, she poured her heart out, saying that she had just been on her knees pleading with the Lord to help her and to let her know that He really was aware of her, that He loved her. Her prayer was literally interrupted by the knock of the one God had sent to answer that petition.

We should actively seek to lift the burdens of others and in so doing become the mortal angels who assist God in answering prayers. The following bit of verse, entitled "Living What We Pray For," is illustrative:

> I knelt to pray when day was done
> And prayed, "O Lord, bless everyone;
> Lift from each saddened heart the pain,
> And let the sick be well again."
> And then I woke another day
> And carelessly went on my way;
> The whole day long, I did not try
> To wipe a tear from any eye.
> I did not try to share the load
> Of any brother on the road;
> I did not even go to see
> The sick man, just next door to me.
> Yet, once again, when day was done,
> I prayed, "O Lord, bless everyone."
> But as I prayed, into my ear
> There came a voice that whispered clear:
> "Pause now, my son, before you pray;
> Whom have you tried to bless today?
> God's sweetest blessings always go
> By hands that serve Him here below."

And then I hid my face and cried,
"Forgive me, God, I have not tried.
Let me but live another day,
And I will live the way I pray."
                    —Whitney Montgomery

Prayers should not be reserved for crises. Elder Howard W. Hunter once noted, "If prayer is only a spasmodic cry at the time of crisis, then it is utterly selfish, and we come to think of God as a repairman or a service agency to help us only in our emergencies" (*Ensign*, Nov. 1977, 52).

Prayer should be a part of our everyday experience. In reality, every moment of our lives is one that matters. The missionary Amulek counseled, "Let your hearts be full, drawn out in prayer unto [God] *continually* for your welfare, and also for the welfare of those who are around you" (Alma 34:27; emphasis added).

We should commence each day in gratitude for yet another day in which to live and learn—and serve. Prayers should continue throughout the day, whether formal or informal, or as the hymn teaches us, "uttered or unexpressed" (*Hymns* [1985], no. 145).

Whether we are working, playing, or studying, there should be a prayer in our hearts. Prayer not only keeps us safe but also improves performance and brings peace of mind.

I learned the importance of prayer as a young missionary. Oh, I had always prayed, but as a child and teenager my prayers had basically been confined to my bedroom and the dinner table. I never gave much attention to the power that prayer could be in my daily activities, such as schoolwork.

When I resumed my university studies following my mission, I began to pray in my heart as I took examinations or participated in classroom exercises and personally experienced the power of prayer. My scholastic performance and grades improved immeasurably because of that added assistance. Prayer should be a vital part of everything we do. I repeat: Every moment matters, and none should be approached without a prayer in our heart.

Some years ago I was happily involved in my chosen profession. I was teaching for the Church Educational System at the Institute of Religion adjacent to the University of Utah, an institution where I had completed my undergraduate degree. I had many fond memories of my years on that campus, for I had been heavily involved in student government, and it was there I had met my eternal companion. I was, therefore, thrilled to be assigned to teach there following a decade of teaching in southern Utah and southern California.

I received a phone call one day inviting me to accept another professional position that would take me out of the classroom and away from the students I so dearly loved. While the offer had appealing aspects, I was reluctant to give up teaching. I finally said, "I'm not sure I want to accept your offer. I'm very happy where I am and in what I am doing." Then the voice at the other end of the phone line asked a penetrating question. The caller said, "Well, *we've* prayed about this decision; why don't *you*!"

That question, which was really in the form of a

declarative statement, and the ensuing prayerful action taken by me, turned my life in another direction full of new growth and experiences.

While the Lord has given us great latitude in exercising our agency, leaving many decisions up to our own judgment, the invitation to counsel with Him "in all [our] doings" (Alma 37:37) should be paramount as we approach any decision.

Young people, in particular, face significant challenges in the daily decisions they must make. We live in a world of changing values and slipping standards. The unacceptable of a few years ago is now common. Followers of Christ must remain true and faithful to His standards. Personal prayer is absolutely essential to making choices that will bring true peace and happiness.

"Prayer is the passport to spiritual power," said President Spencer W. Kimball (*Ensign*, July 1973, 17).

Yes, there is great power in prayer!

"The importance of prayer is emphasized by the fact that the most oft-repeated command given by God to men is to pray," said President Marion G. Romney (*Ensign*, May 1978, 48–49).

The importance of being sincere in prayers is illustrated by the mischievous Huckleberry Finn: "It made me shiver. And I about made up my mind to pray and see if I couldn't try to quit being the kind of boy I was and be better. So I kneeled down. But the words wouldn't come. Why wouldn't they? It weren't no use to try and hide it from Him. . . . I knowed very well why they wouldn't come. It was because my heart warn't right; it was because

I was playing double. I was letting on to give up sin, but away inside of me I was holding on to the biggest one of all. I was trying to make my mouth say I would do the right thing and the clean thing. But deep down in me, I knowed it was a lie, and He knowed it. YOU CAN'T PRAY A LIE. . . . I FOUND THAT OUT" (Mark Twain, *The Adventures of Huckleberry Finn* [New York: Platt & Munk, 1960], 445–46).

Chapter 14

"I Want to Be Good!"

• • • • • • • • •

"You're not one of those *strong* Mormons are you?" The young teenager pondered the question just posed to her. Not quite understanding the meaning behind the taunting query, she responded, "What do you mean?" Her interrogator replied, "You know, one of those families where you have a picture of Jesus hanging on *every* wall in the house!"

What was the intent of the question? Was it really an honest effort on the part of one girl to discover the level of faith of another? Or was it simply a demonstration of the dream of Father Lehi where those who pursue the ways of the world, who are occupying the "great and spacious building," point the finger of scorn at those who are seeking to do what's right! (see 1 Nephi 8:26–27).

Sadly, in today's world there is an ever-increasing tendency of the proud and the so-called popular to put down those who desire to make right choices. These deceivers preach the big lie that it is not "cool" to be good. If you want to be with the "in crowd" then "don't be so uptight," they say. "Don't be a 'Molly Mormon,' a 'goody-goody,' or so 'straight-laced,'" they mock. Even unsavory and degrading labels are also thrown at those who would be good.

Such ridicule is not new. Mockery of goodness has undoubtedly been on this earth from the days of Cain's rebellion. The Book of Mormon records a classic example of the taunting behavior of those who have foolishly turned away from faith and trust in God and who then mock the faithful. "They laughed us to scorn," said the great missionary Ammon when recalling the reaction of the unbelieving to the announcement that he and his brothers were going on their missions (Alma 26:23).

How does one deal effectively with the taunting and ridicule of those who seek to persuade them to be less than their best? Perhaps the simplest and most effective way is just to ignore and quickly dismiss from consideration or discussion such pleadings. Faithful Nephi described just such a response: "Great was the multitude that did enter into that strange building. And after they did enter into that building they did point the finger of scorn at me and those that were partaking of the fruit [of the tree of life] also; but *we heeded them not*" (1 Nephi 8:33; emphasis added).

Our Savior used that same approach when faced with temptations during His mortal life: "He suffered temptations but *gave no heed* unto them" (D&C 20:22; emphasis added).

Each of us would do well to put into action the words of the children's song, "I'm Trying to Be Like Jesus" (*Children's Songbook* [Salt Lake City: The Church of Jesus Christ of Latter-day Saints, 1989], 78). When faced with taunting for holding fast to standards of right, we can gain strength by silently singing these words:

I'm trying to be like Jesus; I'm following in his ways.
I'm trying to love as he did, in all that I do and say.

At times I am tempted to make a wrong choice,
But I try to listen as the still small voice whispers,
Love one another as Jesus loves you.
Try to show kindness in all that you do.
Be gentle and loving in deed and in thought,
For these are the things Jesus taught.

In *all* moments remember who you really are: a son or daughter of God. Knowing your divine origin and considering your divine potential, how could you be less than your best? Many children have heard a loving parent admonish them, "Remember who you are" as they left for an evening with their friends or departed home for some new adventure.

One mother who frequently used that phrase overheard one of her son's friends ask, "Why does your mother always say that to you? What does she mean?" The boy quickly replied, "She means, 'Be good!'" In reflecting on this answer the mother said, "He was exactly right. We remember who we are by doing good, and we do good when we remember who we are" (Susan L. Warner, *Ensign*, May 1996, 79).

One day in a crowded shopping area, a small child was overheard saying, "Am I being good, Daddy?" "Yes," the proud parent replied, "you're being good!"

Oh, how wonderful it would be if in our daily prayers to our divine Parent we could ask, "Am I being good, Father?" and we could hear the response in our hearts and minds, "Yes, my child, you're being good!" Such a regular response would assure that one day we would hear those welcome words, "Well done, thou good and faithful servant: thou hast been faithful . . . enter thou into the joy of thy lord" (Matthew 25:21).

A desire to be good may come not only from remembering our divine origin and nature but also from considering our earthly heritage. For example, consider the counsel of a loving father to two of his children. Each had been given a first name of a worthy ancestor. Said the father:

"Behold, I have given unto you the names of our first parents who came out of the land of Jerusalem; and this I have done that when you remember your names ye may remember them; and when ye remember them ye may remember their works; and when ye remember their works ye may know how that it is said, and also written, that *they were good*.

"Therefore, my sons, I would that ye should do that which is good, that it may be said of you, and also written, even as it has been said and written of them" (Helaman 5:6–7; emphasis added).

Now, even if your name may not have any special connection to an illustrious ancestor, *you* can make that name special to your posterity by your choices *now*. Live so as to leave a legacy of good works and an honorable name to your children, grandchildren, and future posterity. Let your name—first, middle, and last—be honored because you were good.

One of the great leaders of our dispensation is President Boyd K. Packer. This mighty apostle of great faith has left his mark for good not only on his own posterity, but he has also blessed members of the Church throughout the world through his inspired counsel and teachings. As a young man he made a critical choice. He determined he wanted to be good. He said, "I went before [the Lord] and in essence said, 'I'm not neutral, and You can do with me what You want. If You need my voice, it's there. I don't care what You do with me, and You don't have to take anything from me because I give it to You—everything, all I own, all I am.'"

"I desire to be good," he declared. "Some people would be ashamed to say that, but I am not. I want to be good. I want to be a good father. I want to be a good servant of our Heavenly Father. I want to be a good brother, a good husband. That is not easy. I sometimes fall short, but when I do, I have a steady grip for which I reach. I cling to one rod that relates to the decision about wanting to be good" (*That All May Be Edified* [Salt Lake City: Bookcraft, 1982], 259).

Think of the immeasurable loss to the Packer posterity, to members of The Church of Jesus Christ of Latter-day Saints, and to countless others throughout the world that would have occurred had the young Boyd K. Packer not made the decision to be good.

I share one small but significant example of the rippling effects of this decision by President Packer. While I was serving as a mission president in the Netherlands and Belgium, one of our missionaries informed me that he had decided to leave the mission field and return home. There was no transgression involved in his decision. He just felt unsure about the depth of his testimony. He decided a mission was not worth giving up several years of his life. I prayerfully counseled with him for some time, but he remained resolute in his decision.

Then one of those promptings to which the servants of the Lord are entitled came to me. I reached up on my personal library shelf and took down a book I had brought with me into the mission field. It was a volume filled with the inspired writings of President Packer. I did not have any particular chapter in mind as I handed him the book but merely said, "Elder, I feel impressed to ask you to read this book. If after you have read it you still want to return home, I won't stand in your way. However, I feel there is something in these writings that will change your mind."

Several weeks later I received a phone call from the elder and was thrilled to hear him say, "President, thank you for letting me read that book. You were right! I did find something that helped me, and I have decided to stay on my mission."

How different the future of that young missionary might have been if that book had never been written, if Boyd K. Packer had not made a decision to be good.

Being good pertains not only to righteousness but also to our efforts in all aspects of our lives. Elder Spencer J. Condie has wisely counseled, "Our Father in Heaven not only wants you to be good, but to be good for something, to serve and bless the lives of others, and to become a benefit to your fellow beings" (*Ensign*, May 2002, 44).

Being good means being your best, but it does not mean you are in competition to be better than someone else. Unlike mortal measurements such as grading curves, the Lord will not measure your performance against that of another, but only against what you yourself were capable of doing.

The legendary basketball coach John Wooden, whose teams won ten national championships and had four undefeated seasons, was taught a great lesson early in his life about striving to be his personal best. "Don't worry much about trying to be better than someone else," his father said. "Learn from others, yes. But don't just try to be better than they are. You have no control over that. Instead try, and try very hard, to be the best that you can be. That you have control over" (http://www.coachwooden.com/bodysuccess.shml).

Elder Marvin J. Ashton once observed, "One of the finest presents you can give anyone is your best self" (*Ensign*, Jan. 1973, 43). How can I be my best self unless I want to be good!

This principle may be illustrated in the story of Eliza Doolittle, the heroine of *My Fair Lady*, who was transformed from a socially inept, plain, and lowly flower lady into a strikingly beautiful and confident woman. While much credit for this miraculous metamorphosis may be given to Eliza's mentor, Professor Henry Higgins, an underlying basis of her transformation was her frequently cited (and practiced) declaration, "I'm a good girl, I am!"

We, too, have the potential of a magnificent and miraculous transformation, for the promise is given that in the resurrection "shall the righteous *shine* forth in the kingdom of God" (Alma 40:25; emphasis added). Those whose goodness and obedience in following and keeping the ordinances, covenants, and commandments of the restored gospel of Jesus Christ qualify themselves to return to live in the presence of our Father in Heaven and His Beloved Son in the celestial kingdom. Such righteous individuals will be clothed with celestial bodies that will be glorious beyond description (see D&C 88:28).

Do you want to live in everlasting joy? Then in mortal moments that may be so defining, choose righteousness. Declare yourself to be good in *desire*, in *word*, in *thought*, and in *action*.

Chapter 15

YOU MAKE THE
DECISION

◆　◆　◆　◆　◆　◆　◆　◆　◆

"Wherefore, men are free . . . to choose liberty and eternal life, through the great Mediator of all men, or to choose captivity and death, according to the captivity and power of the devil" (2 Nephi 2:27).

The right to make choices—free agency—is at the heart of God's plan for us here on earth. A pre-earthly war was waged over this very principle, as Satan "sought to destroy the agency of man" (Moses 4:3). Should man have the freedom to choose his course of action, or should he be forced to follow a prescribed path? We voted to follow the Father's plan, in which choices are available through the exercise of moral agency. But so, too, are the inevitable consequences of those choices.

Elder William R. Bradford made the following observations on this issue: "The most basic, fundamental principle of truth, that upon which the entire plan of God is founded, is free agency. As an individual you have the right to govern yourself. It is divinely given to you to think and act as you wish. It is your decision.

"It must be pointed out, however, that *although you have the free agency to choose for yourself, you do not have the right to choose what will be the result of your decision.* The results of what you think and do are governed by law. Good returns good. Evil returns evil. You govern yourself by subjecting yourself to the discipline of law. If you are obedient to God's law, you remain free. You progress and are perfected. If you are disobedient to God's law, you bind yourself to that which restricts your progress. You become defiled and unworthy to be an associate with those who are more clean and pure" (*Ensign*, Nov. 1979, 37; emphasis added).

When Elder Robert D. Hales received a call from the First Presidency to serve as a mission president, he was asked five questions. Concerning this experience, Elder Hales said, "On any one of those five questions, had I had to give a no I would have lost my free agency" ("A Question of Free Agency," *Ensign*, May 1975, 43). His affirmative response to each of these questions led not only to his call as a mission president but also to his call to serve as a General Authority.

When we are faced with a decision about which of two choices to make, we should ask ourselves a simple question: Which of these two choices will bring me closer to the illuminating light and peaceful presence of my Heavenly Father and the Savior, and which of the two choices might draw me toward the devil and his despair and darkness?

The choice should be relatively simple when we remember that God's goals for us are that we obtain a fulness of joy and become as he is (see 2 Nephi 2:25; 3 Nephi 28:10; D&C 52:43; Moses 1:39). On the other hand, the devil's desire is that we become as miserable and wretched as he is, for "he rewardeth you no good thing" (Alma 34:39; see also 2 Nephi 2:18, 27; Alma 30:60).

Prophets on two continents anciently admonished the people with sound counsel that still applies as we consider choices: "Choose ye this day, whom ye will serve" (Alma 30:8; Joshua 24:15).

Elder Neal A. Maxwell, a modern-day apostle, once added this counsel to these inspired words: "Joshua didn't say 'choose you next year whom you will serve;' he spoke of 'this day,' while there is still daylight and before the darkness becomes more and more normal" (Conference Report, Oct. 1974, 15).

Once we have made a firm, unalterable decision to follow God, then there is no future debate. Our course of action is charted. There are no exceptions in a moment of temptation for those who have made sacred covenants and keep their commitments.

Many years ago, before he was called as a member of the Quorum of the Twelve Apostles, Spencer W. Kimball was in France on a business trip. He attended a banquet where seven goblets of colorful wine were poured at every place setting. As he sat there, far from home and those who knew of his standards, he seemed to hear satanic whisperings: "This is your chance. You are thousands of miles from home. There is no one here to watch you. No one will ever know if you drink the contents of those goblets. This is your chance!"

Then came the sweeter, soothing whisperings of the still, small voice: "You have a covenant with yourself: you promised yourself you would never do it; and with your Heavenly Father you made a covenant, and you have gone these years without breaking it, and you would be stupid to break this covenant after all these years."

When the banquet was over, the glasses of colorful liquid by his plate remained untouched. Spencer W. Kimball had been true to the decision of his youth to follow the Father of our spirits (see Conference Report, Apr. 1974, 127).

When we have made the choice to follow God under all circumstances, to make absolutely *no* exceptions, the voice of the tempter has no swaying power.

Contrast the above experience with the tragic results that came to a family because a man had not made an irrevocable decision to be true. The man had been a slave to alcohol most of his life but had finally been persuaded to free himself from his bondage to the bottle. Through the exercise of self-control, and the help of loving friends and family, he quit his drinking and began the process that would take him to the holy temple with his loved ones.

The day finally arrived when, recommends in hand, he and his family drove to the temple for the sealing that would bind them together as an eternal unit. They arrived early, and the husband and wife went their separate ways to take care of some errands. Unfortunately, he ran into some old acquaintances who urged him to come to the tavern for a *friendly drink*. At first he was firm in his rejection of their offer. But then they persuaded him to join them for just a soft drink. He wouldn't have to drink alcohol, they said, just come and be friendly—for "old time's sake!" Surely no harm could come from this.

Several hours later, an intoxicated, broken man met

his deeply disappointed wife. The commitment had not been kept. The temple experience was canceled. The blessings were lost. All was ruined because a man had not made an unalterable decision to follow the standard of God and keep his covenants. He had allowed others to detour his initial decision to do good (see Spencer W. Kimball, *The Miracle of Forgiveness* [Salt Lake City: Bookcraft, 1969], 170–71).

Those who would try to persuade us to bend *just a little*, to vacillate and violate standards, are *not* friends. They may feign friendship, but they should be recognized for the wolves of prey that they are. Perhaps the warning of the Savior could be appropriately altered to state, "*Beware of false [friends]*, which come to you in sheep's clothing, but inwardly they are ravening wolves" (Matthew 7:15; emphasis added).

A friend is one who lifts and inspires us to high standards. In defining moments, the character of true friends will be easily seen. The kiss of Judas, though offered in the guise of friendship, was a self-seeking and treacherous betrayal of trust (see Luke 22:47–48). The Savior pointed out that the *love* of a friend is evidenced in his desire to save his friend's life (see John 15:13). A true friend would not seek to rob another of his *eternal* life by leading him astray.

Occasionally the wolves who pretend to be friends play on sympathy or past loyalty. An outstanding Latter-day Saint high school student began dating an older student whose standards were far below hers. At first she was unaware of the differences in their values. She was attracted to the young man, and he carefully spun a web of deceit that trapped her emotionally. She soon realized the true character of her would-be friend and broke off further dating and contact.

The boy pleaded that they have "one last date" together. After all, he argued, they had been such good friends, and he was despondent over their breakup. "Besides, I have changed!" he said. She sought the advice of her seminary teacher, who strongly counseled her not to succumb to the pressure of this ploy to get her entangled in the boy's web once again. Unfortunately, her emotions and sympathies overcame her reason and resolve. She thought she could help him by going with him this "one last time." The barrier was broken and, like a helpless lamb, she was carried off by this wolf to the lair of his lifestyle. Today she remains outside the fold of the true Shepherd.

There is a striking difference between this girl's experience and that of another young member of the Church. One night he was asked by a friend to accompany him, his girlfriend, and her sister to the girl's home. Shortly after arriving at the house, the girl he was with turned off the lights, sat on the young man's lap, and started making advances.

The young man, who was a priest in the Aaronic Priesthood, knew he was in a dangerous situation. Like Joseph of old, his character was being tested by a modern-day Potiphar's wife (see Genesis 39:11–12). The boy was as true as Joseph. He made the unpopular decision to resist. Excusing himself, he left the girl's house and returned to the safety of his own home. Many years later he was called to serve as one of the General Authorities of the Church. In relating this story to President N. Eldon Tanner, he recalled, "I shudder to think what might have happened if I had stayed with her and have concluded many times that I might never have been here as a servant of the Lord" (Conference Report, Oct. 1975, 114–15).

Few will ever be called to serve as General Authorities or hold other highly visible positions of trust and leadership. But holding such positions is not the gauge by which God will measure our righteousness. Elder Bruce R. McConkie reminded us that "blessings come because of obedience and personal righteousness, not because of administrative positions" (in Spencer W. Kimball et al., *Priesthood* [Salt Lake City: Deseret Book, 1981], 30).

Although we may not choose the positions in which we can render service in this life, all may choose to make righteous decisions. In a similar vein, we may not always have the liberty to choose the circumstances that control our lives, but we do have the *freedom* to choose our reactions to each situation we face. A marvelous example of this principle is seen in the life of a Polish man during World War II.

When the war finally ended, the hated gates of concentration camps were opened to free the abused and emaciated victims of enemy cruelty. Many of these victims were themselves now filled with hatred toward their captors and others. Unfortunately, this vengeful feeling created an inner conflict that raged long after the external war had ceased its hostilities. However, among the victims disgorged from the bowels of these wretched camps, there was one man from Poland who was different. He had such a presence of peace about him that some mistakenly thought he had only recently been incarcerated and had not yet had time to become like most of the other hapless prisoners.

Upon questioning him, however, it was discovered that he had suffered terrible atrocities inflicted by heartless invaders. The man had been forced to watch in horror as soldiers had lined up his wife, two daughters, and three small sons against a wall and cruelly shot them to death with machine-gun fire. He had begged to die with his family, but he had been kept alive because of his language ability and potential usefulness to these enemies of his homeland.

At this point he had to make a choice. He said, "I had to decide right then . . . whether to let myself hate the soldiers who had done this. It was an easy decision, really. I was a lawyer. In my practice I had seen . . . what hate could do to people's minds and bodies. Hate had just killed the six people who mattered most to me in the world. I decided then that I would spend the rest of my life— whether it was a few days or many years—loving every person I came in contact with" (George G. Ritchie with Elizabeth Sherrill, *Return from Tomorrow* [Grand Rapids, Mich.: Chosen Books, n.d.], 116).

"I say unto you, Love your enemies, bless them that curse you, do good to them that hate you, and pray for them which despitefully use you, and persecute you" (Matthew 5:44).

In a defining moment, a man who had such mortal justification for hating others decided not to allow himself to become yet another victim of cruelty. Instead he chose to follow the counsel of the One who himself exemplified the principle of returning good for evil. When we are tempted to say, "You make me angry," or "You are the reason for my misconduct or bad attitude," it would be well to remember the example of the Polish man and the counsel of the Son of Man.

Remember, *you* make the decision!

Occasionally we surrender values and beliefs to the temptation or punishment inflicted by invaders and would-be conquerors of a different nature. The Lord warned that there would be "conspiring men in the last days" who would have evil designs in their hearts (D&C 89:4). Although this warning is couched in the revelation known as the Word of Wisdom, it is not restricted to those who promote the use of harmful substances such as alcohol, tobacco, and drugs.

A plague of pornography has spread throughout the world because of *conspiring men* whose evil design is to flaunt filth for profit. If we allow this type of enemy to enter our lives, we surrender our souls to the evil one. Sometimes it creeps in subtly through an off-color joke. Listening to such stories can stain the soul just as surely as looking at a pornographic picture. Filth is filth, and we make the choice as to whether we will post a No Trespassing sign to stop pollution or allow its corrosive influence to contaminate our spirits.

A graduation party was held at the end of a school

year. Unfortunately, it was the kind of party that "sneaked into the lineup" of otherwise well-planned parties. Several vulgar movies were to be shown, but the participants invited to the party did not know this before arriving. Once the movies started, the filth became apparent. Some courageous young people got up and left, while others, either out of prurient curiosity or peer pressure for popularity, remained. Once outside, those who had decided to keep their minds unpolluted found others just arriving and informed them of the nature of the party. Once again, choices were made. Some decided to leave, while the weak chose to join the party, there to be "polluted by the power of Satan."

Commenting on this experience, Bishop H. Burke Peterson observed, "It's worth doing whatever we must to be approved by the Lord" (Conference Report, Oct. 1974, 97).

As was the case in our pre-earthly existence, there will be those weak ones who choose to follow the lures of Lucifer and be led into his snares. Yet there will always be those faithful followers of our Heavenly Father and the Savior. In defining moments each of us is faced with the decision as to whom we will follow. So much depends on that choice.

In 1960 Elder Harold B. Lee attended a meeting of missionaries in The Hague, Holland. He told the elders that life was like a football game. When the ball has been advanced to the last ten yards, both teams put in their most effective players. One team will have its smartest offensive unit using their best strategy to score a touchdown, while the other team will have its toughest defensive unit on the field of action.

Elder Lee said the world's history had reached the ten-yard line and the end of the game was near. The Lord has reserved some of his most valiant spirits to come to earth at this time and make the touchdown for him. On the other hand, Lucifer has marshaled his most wicked forces and brought forth his most evil schemes to try to stop the Lord's team from succeeding. The fight between good and evil is very real, and the Lord is counting on the members of His team to do their best, to choose the correct game plan.

No position is unimportant; each has a vital role. The words of Mordecai to Queen Esther at a decisive moment in their nation's history have appropriate application to each of us: "Who knoweth whether thou are come to the kingdom for such a time as this?" (Esther 4:14).

As you consider your present and future choices, remember who you are as a son or daughter of God. The choices you make matter very much. Each will either bring you closer to your Father in Heaven, to become more like Him, or draw you away to the dark side.

"Every time you make a choice you are turning the central part of you, the part of you that chooses, into something a little different from what it was before. And taking your life as a whole, with all your innumerable choices, all your life long you are slowly turning this central thing either into a heavenly creature or into a hellish creature" (C. S. Lewis, *Mere Christianity* [New York: Macmillan, 1943], 86).

INDEX

◆ ◆ ◆ ◆ ◆ ◆ ◆ ◆ ◆ ◆

love of God as the force behind, 107; story of young woman responding to Gordon B. Hinckley's counsel on pierced earrings, 107–8; M. Russell Ballard on obeying the prophet, 108; story of woman objecting to Harold B. Lee's counsel on beards for men, 108; following the living prophet, 108–9; Ezra Taft Benson on following the living prophet, 109; Joseph Smith on, 109; children's song about, 109–10; story about football players breaking team rules, 110; Joseph B. Wirthlin on, 111, 112; story of Creed Haymond, 111–12; Gordon B. Hinckley on, 112; Bruce R. McConkie on, 165

O'Brien, Pat, 44–45

Officers' training school banquet, story of young man at, 37–38

One, power of: Gordon B. Hinckley on letting your voice be heard, 9; importance of speaking up, 9, 10, 19–20; experience of Vaughn J. Featherstone at post-basketball game party, 9–10; story of young man befriending suicidal young woman, 10–11; looking beyond yourself, 11–12; story of adulterous young soldier, 12; being your brother's keeper, 12–13; story of shoemaker introducing mother of John A. Widtsoe to Gospel, 13–14; story of missionary at wedding ceremony, 14–15; story of young woman objecting to incorrect doctrine in school assembly, 16; story of young man objecting to incorrect doctrine taught by

school teacher, 16–17; experience of Rex D. Pinegar hearing brother chastise friend for using profanity, 17–18; Neal A. Maxwell on being a stern sentinel, 18; experience on bus with boys using profanity, 18–19; Neal A. Maxwell on being bound by principle, 20

Opposition, overcoming. *See* Adversity, responding to

Pace, Glenn L., experience failing in athletics, 63–65

Pacheo, Ruben Dario, 6–7

Packer, Boyd K., 73–74; on obedience, 104; on following promptings of the Spirit, 120–21; experience in lost warplane, 121–22; as an example of being good, 154–56; on being good, 155

Palacio, Bobby, 85–86

Paralyzed University of Utah gymnast, story of, 60–61

Paramore, James M., 122

Passing out in BYU cafeteria, story about young man, 22

Perry, L. Tom, 81–82

Peterson, H. Burke: experience swallowing plastic tube, 129–31; on prayer and following promptings, 130–31; on being approved by the Lord, 168

Phone book, experience of young missionary picking name from, 124–25

Pilate, 113–14

Pinegar, Lynn, 17–18

Pinegar, Rex D., 25–26; experience hearing brother chastise friend for using profanity, 17–18; experience making commitment to academic excellence, 47–48